Creative Love

10 WAYS TO BUILD
A FUN AND LASTING LOVE

JEREMY & AUDREY ROLOFF

ZONDERVAN®

ZONDERVAN

Creative Love: 10 Ways to Build a Fun and Lasting Love

© 2021 Jeremy and Audrey Roloff

Requests for information should be addressed to:
Zondervan, *3900 Sparks Dr. SE, Grand Rapids, Michigan 49546*

ISBN 978-0-310-09646-7
ISBN 978-0-310-45681-0 (audiobook)
ISBN 978-0-310-45198-3 (eBook)

Scripture quotations marked ESV are from the ESV® Bible (The Holy Bible, English Standard Version®). Copyright © 2001 by Crossway, a publishing ministry of Good News Publishers. Used by permission. All rights reserved.

Scripture quotations marked NASB are from the New American Standard Bible®. Copyright © 1960, 1962, 1963, 1968, 1971, 1972, 1973, 1975, 1977, 1995 by The Lockman Foundation. Used by permission. (www.Lockman.org)

Scripture quotations marked NIV are from the Holy Bible, New International Version®, NIV®. Copyright © 1973, 1978, 1984, 2011 by Biblica, Inc.® Used by permission of Zondervan. All rights reserved worldwide. www.zondervan.com. The "NIV" and "New International Version" are trademarks registered in the United States Patent and Trademark Office by Biblica, Inc.®

Scripture quotations marked NKJV are from the New King James Version®. © 1982 by Thomas Nelson. Used by permission. All rights reserved.

Scripture quotations marked NLT are from the Holy Bible, New Living Translation. © 1996, 2004, 2007, 2013 by Tyndale House Foundation. Used by permission of Tyndale House Publishers, Inc., Carol Stream, Illinois 60188. All rights reserved.

Any Internet addresses (websites, blogs, etc.) and telephone numbers in this book are offered as a resource. They are not intended in any way to be or imply an endorsement by Zondervan, nor does Zondervan vouch for the content of these sites and numbers for the life of this book.

The authors are represented by Alive Literary Agency, 7680 Goddard Street, Suite 200, Colorado Springs, Colorado 80920, www.aliveliterary.com.

Cover photo © Dawn Jarvis/Dawn Photography LLC
Photos © Brian Schindler, 2020, www.brianschindler.co: pages 118, 147
Photos © Dawn Jarvis/Dawn Photography LLC: pages 5, 48, 58, 68, 115, 121, 145, 184, 195, 200
Photos © Jeremy Roloff: pages 17, 21, 23, 28, 32, 45, 63, 73, 77, 79, 83, 93, 125, 128, 139, 140, 179, 181
Photos © Monique Serra Photography: pages 53, 59, 106, 108, 165, 175
Photos © Shutterstock: page 15 by Vira Mylyan-Monastyrska, page 160 by Gena96, page 198 by Bartek Zyczynski
Photos © Unsplash: pages 7, 16, 40, 70, 86, 98, 99, 132, 136, 154, 155, 159, 170, 173, 187

Art direction: Jen Greenwalt
Interior design: Tiffany Forrester and Mallory Collins

Printed in China

20 21 22 23 24 DSC 10 9 8 7 6 5 4 3 2 1

Contents

A Letter to the Reader vii

Chapter 1. Words That Weave 1
Creative Communication That Strengthens and Heals

Chapter 2. Suspense, Spontaneity, and Surprise 19
Take Your Love on an Adventure

Chapter 3. Strands of Togetherness 41
The Principle of Sharing

Chapter 4. Lock It In 61
Making Memories and Marking Moments

Chapter 5. Pomp and Circumstance 81
Making the Most of Special Occasions

Chapter 6. Two to Tango 101
How to Creatively Navigate Conflict

Chapter 7. The Joy of Generosity 119
Giving Creative Gifts

Chapter 8. Play Dates and Date Nights. 137
    Wanna Go Out with Me?

Chapter 9. A Lifetime Warranty. 157
    Safeguarding Your Love Story

Chapter 10. Dreaming Together 177
    Casting Vision, Crafting Your Mission, and
    Committing to Your Values

Notes. 197

About the Authors 199

A Letter to the Reader

Friend,

We invite you to join us as we seek a love that is creative in its pursuit, its intention, and its actions. When we look to Christ as the example for how to love one another, we see how creativity is the heartbeat of lasting love. God loves us unconditionally, and He reveals His unchanging love for us in creative new ways—through His creation, a well-timed word, a compelling question, the cadence of a song, His living Word, a treasured friendship, a satisfying meal, a child full of wonder, a heart-swelling memory, an epic adventure, or even the pages of a book. We offer you these pages full of creative ideas, questions, and challenges with the hope of helping you build a fun, fulfilling, and forever love.

Our prayer is that these words will guide you into more meaningful conversations and inspire you to think of unique-to-you ways to love your significant other. This book is an invitation, not a prescription. And, full disclosure, we by no means consider ourselves experts when it comes to relationships. But we are passionate about marriage, and we trust that God can use our stories and the things we've learned to inspire and encourage you in writing your own love story. Our marriage is full of imperfections, but we hope that sharing our creative solutions for when we mess up, fall short, and need grace will lead you to the same life-giving love we have experienced from God and each other.

After seeing the response to our first book, *A Love Letter Life*, we wanted to expand on some of the concepts we discussed and offer practical tools for how to invest in your relationship. While *A Love Letter Life* focused heavily on our story from our first date to "I do," this book focuses on pivotal moments from every stage of our relationship—from dating to marriage to our growing family—and shares new revelations and helpful lessons we've learned from older, wiser couples who have generously imparted their insight to us.

These ten ways apply creativity to central aspects of a dating or marriage relationship. Each chapter is intended to spark conversations, pose questions, and invite you into love-strengthening practices. For that reason, we hope you don't read the chapters all at once and then put the book on a shelf; instead, we encourage you to see this as a timeless resource you can refer to as your relationship grows. Whether you are currently dating and falling in love, engaged and preparing for marriage, or married and protecting your promise, you have a unique love story. We hope this book inspires you to keep on writing it in even more creative ways!

Under the mercy,

Jeremy and Audrey Roloff

Chapter 1

WORDS THAT
WEAVE

*Creative Communication That
Strengthens and Heals*

Gracious words are like a honeycomb,
sweetness to the soul and health to the body.

PROVERBS 16:24 ESV

Jeremy and I met on January 16, 2010, when I answered the door for our first (blind) date in my sports bra and running shorts, soaking wet and covered in mud. Apparently Jeremy sees past first impressions. Life has changed slightly between then and now. I currently am nestled in with our newborn son, Bode, while his two-year-old sister, Ember, is babbling away, "reading" her books in front of the fire. Normally we plan something special every January 16 to celebrate the day we met, but life has its seasons, and this one is keeping us from our regular traditions. But as one tradition fades, it makes space for a new one, so I picked up a piece of paper and a pen.

As I sat down to write a letter to Jeremy, I thought back on the past ten years of our relationship, praying as I wrote. I felt so much joy in reflecting on those years and realizing how he has changed since that first day. I spent some time thinking about a word to describe Jeremy for every year over the last decade. The words that emerged described the ways I have seen him grow year after year. The practice endeared my heart toward my best friend, and I could see on Jeremy's face how my words affected him. Later when I asked him what he thought about that letter, he responded, "I remember thinking, 'Wow, you noticed all that?' To know that you are watching, learning, and appreciating who I am and who I am becoming surfaced several feelings all at once—love, joy, encouragement, and conviction—and it reminded me that who I am becoming matters."

Our entire dating relationship was long distance, and we found a few practices that sealed our love while we were apart—creativity, intentionality, letter writing, and discovering new things about each other. Ten years in, we've discovered that those same practices are crucial to sustaining and growing our relationship. It took work then, and it takes work now, but the reward is so worth it! Now that we're married, working together, and raising kids, there are more demands on our time, and getting creative with our words requires extra effort, but it's still an incredibly important part of keeping our relationship strong.

We aren't perfect, and we've experienced when a careless word tears the bonds of a relationship, when the absence of a needed word erodes it, and when a word spoken out of spite or bitterness does damage. However, we know that *even more powerful* are timely words spoken with respect, intention, and sincerity. Words that illuminate the soul and affirm the person we do life with not only heal past wounds but also serve as protection against future hurts. When we speak truth over our loved ones, our words can serve to weave us together in a way that creates strength, resilience, endurance, and deep joy.

We want to share some creative ways to use the power of words, whether they come in the form of a text, a poem, a love letter, or a simple "I love you" spoken from the heart. The good news is that you don't have to be gifted with words for this to make your love stronger; it's the planning, intention, and regularity behind those words that speak the loudest.

Love Letters

AUDREY: If you've been following our story for a while, you know Jeremy and I have a thing for letters. Yes, *letters*. Real pen and ink on paper, folded into stamped envelopes. As I mentioned before, our entire dating relationship was long distance, and we wrote letters back and forth over those three years—Jer writing many of his letters to me on an old-fashioned typewriter. We wanted *more* than text messages and nightly phone calls. We had a deep desire to add excitement and creativity to our communication. Letters seemed perfect.

We believe that creative words spoken to or about your love can breathe so much life into your relationship. So we've kept letter writing at the center of our love story. We write them every year on our anniversary to be read the following year. We write them before significant moments or on special occasions. And we write them when we need to apologize. (An acknowledgement of wrongdoing and

a request for forgiveness in writing simply conveys greater sincerity.) Sometimes the letters are pages long, and other times they're sticky-note love messages.

For my birthday one year, after we were married, Jeremy bought me a pretty glass jar. Attached to it was a birthday card that explained why he was gifting me such an odd and seemingly meaningless object. He said that he was committing to write me a little love note every night. That jar represented a promise; it would contain a year's worth of his love for me. Every night for an entire year he wrote me one-sentence love letters of encouragement, affirmation, or gratitude, and he would place them on my pillow while I was getting ready for bed. I would read them and smile and then place them in the jar. There was something so powerful about *reading* the words; the physical ink on paper seemed to give Jeremy's genuine words substance and permanence. I fell asleep feeling encouraged and cherished every night because of those love notes.

Physical ink on paper gives genuine words substance and permanence.

A couple of years later, enter our first kid. I was longing for some notes on my pillow. It was a busy season for us, and we would often go to bed talking about work or schedules. I missed those sweet moments of connection that the nightly notes offered. So I found a cute mailbox from Pottery Barn and ordered it. Then I bought some pink and blue craft paper and cut it up into little strips so that when we look back through the notes, we can quickly distinguish who wrote each one. When the mailbox arrived, Jer opened the box (anyone else's husband open all the packages?) and brought it into the kitchen with a confused look on his face. I was giddy to explain my idea. I told him how I wanted to bring back the nightly notes, but this time I wanted to write them too! Jer loved the idea, and we hung the mailbox in our bedroom for what we called our "mailbox affirmations." I put

the pink slips of paper in my nightstand drawer, and Jer put the blue ones in his. We started leaving notes on each other's pillow every night. It was so fun to be able to do this for Jer since I never reciprocated when he did it an entire year for me (oops, lame wife award).

We were really good about doing this every night in the beginning, and though now we do it more sporadically, it's still a nightly invitation to exchange words of encouragement, affirmation, and gratitude. I love the nights when we remember, because we both end the day feeling seen, appreciated, encouraged, and loved. Those simple little ripped-up construction-paper notes have seasoned our love with affection.

Passing Notes

AUDREY: Passing notes like we're in middle school can seem like a little thing. But it's the little things that count. And sometimes those little things become the big things. Yes, we love writing letters even today, years into our marriage. But we've realized that even a single text is a simple action that can go a long way. With our phones, we have the power to use words to inspire, encourage, romance, and love each other at any moment of any day! You may not have the time to plan some big elaborate date night, or perhaps you don't have the money to buy your love a fancy gift, but you *can* send a thoughtful text message to turn their day around.

During our first year of marriage, my job required me to wake up at 2:30 A.M. and commute from West Hollywood (where we lived) to Pasadena (where I worked) and then work until 1:00 P.M. I worked in sales for a wine distributor, managing a bunch of accounts in the Pasadena area. My days consisted of physically demanding work, grumpy people who worked the night shift, cutthroat competition, and getting told no all day long. I'm sure many of you can relate to working a job like this, the kind that seems relentlessly discouraging. Anyone?

Every morning at around 9:00 A.M. (the average human's morning, that is), halfway through my workday, I would feel my phone buzz in my work slacks. It would be a text from Jeremy. Without fail, he would send me an encouraging note—sometimes just a few words long. His daily texts gave me the motivation to keep on going, to stay confident, and to be thankful, and they reminded me that I'm loved. More than that, his messages made me excited to be home with him every night. Sometimes he would put sticky notes that had little encouraging messages in my car, in my work binder, or on the bathroom mirror. Every time I found one, a shameless smile spread across my face. Since my sales job was very competitive and I felt rejected or torn down a lot, Jer's sticky-note affirmations infused a jolt of joy to my days.

On the weekends when Jeremy was away working on a photo shoot or filming a wedding, I would return the favor. Sometimes I would slip a note into his camera bag before he left. We were, and are, always looking for new ways to encourage each other, build each other's confidence, and reiterate our love. Moments spent apart are some of the most powerful opportunities to create a stronger bond with your loved one. Don't waste them!

20 LOVE TEXTS

To help you love, romance, encourage,
and flirt with each other

1. I am so proud of you, and I am proud to call you mine.
2. I was just listening to _____(song), and it reminded me of when _____.
3. Being with you brings me peace and joy.
4. I love you, and I love who you are becoming.
5. I have a surprise for you when we see each other! (Get a little gift you know they'll love.)
6. I'm sitting here wishing I could kiss you right now.
7. Did you know that you have the most handsome/beautiful _____?
8. (Send an old photo of the two of you and write out why you love what the photo represents.)
9. You look goooood, babe. (This is especially fun if you are across the room from each other at an event.)

10. I just arranged for a babysitter for tonight. May I take you on a date?

11. I made your favorite meal! (Send a photo.)

12. I believe in you, _____. You are going to do great things!

13. I love doing life with you. We make the best team!

14. (Write your love story in three sentences, followed by "We have a great love story.")

15. (Send a list of five things you love about them, specific to this week.)

16. (If your significant other is comfortable with social media, post a photo and tell people why you love your person, then send them a screenshot.)

17. (Send them a Bible verse that would encourage them.)

18. (Send them a flirty GIF that will make them laugh.)

19. (Quote a line from their favorite movie but with your own creative spin.)

20. (Send them a prayer in an audio message.)

Seeds of Affirmation

JEREMY: Words are powerful. How you speak and what you say to your beloved matters. It's possible that you know your person better than anyone else does. You know what lies they are tempted to believe and what truths they need to be reminded of. A relationship is like a garden: loving nourishment, like water and sun, are crucial, and protection from pests and uninvited growth is critical! That means you have the power to yank the lies from your beloved's life and replace them with words of truth. If you don't yank the weeds, they will prevent the flowers from flourishing. If we don't sow seeds of affirmation and tend to the garden consistently, it will be overwhelming to tend to when we finally get around to it. We can't let our relationship be something that we finally get around to tending.

The words you speak to your loved one—both from afar and in person—can nourish your relationship by instilling specific truths in their heart and mind. Try looking your partner in the eye and sharing something you

> A relationship is like a garden; we have the power to uproot lies from each other's lives and regularly sow seeds of truth. Don't let your relationship be something that you finally get around to tending.

know will bring them life. Or whisper those words in their ear when you know they are feeling discouraged. Whether or not your primary love language is "words of affirmation," we all need to be encouraged and affirmed through words of truth spoken by the people we love.

Here are a few things we think *she* needs to hear and *he* needs to hear. (Audrey came up with the list for the ladies, and I came up with the list for the men.) We hope these truths help to weave a more tight-knit love story and inspire you to come up with your own!

Things *She* Needs to Hear

1. You are worthy.
2. I'm proud of you.
3. Thank you for everything you do for me.
4. You are gorgeous.
5. I trust you.
6. You are respected by so many.
7. Thank you for sharing what's on your heart with me.
8. I love pursuing you.
9. Your friends are blessed to have you in their lives.
10. How can I help you today?
11. You impress me, and watching you inspires me.

12. How can I love you better?
13. Don't worry. I'll fix it!
14. I have learned a lot from you.
15. I love calling you mine.

Things *He* Needs to Hear

1. I trust you.
2. I appreciate when you _____.
3. You are handsome.
4. Thank you for fixing that.
5. I respect you.
6. I'm thankful you're my man.
7. I'm so glad we're together.
8. You are so good at _____.
9. You make me feel safe.
10. You're a good leader. I trust where you are leading us.
11. You're capable.
12. You are fun to be with.
13. I am with you on this.
14. I was impressed with how you handled that situation.
15. I support your decision.

Of course, this is just a brief list designed to get you started, but try asking your beloved what they need to hear. Then be open and generous with your words—especially when you know they're having a hard time with something. Don't be afraid of sounding cheesy. Sometimes the things we think will be the cheesiest end up being the most impactful. Choose courage over fear! Love invites risk, and sometimes giving voice to your words is nerve-racking as we resist feeling stupid, possible rejection, or passivity from the one we love. Change up the form in which you communicate words of affirmation, whether it's spoken, written, texted, voicemailed, or sent in the mail, and pay attention to their response!

That said, next time a loving thought about your special someone comes to mind, externalize it. Take a chance and transform unspoken thoughts into creative words. You never know how significant they might be to the one you love. We still treasure those letters we sent each other when we were first dating—in fact, they'd probably be among the first things we'd grab if our house were on fire! The closeness they created and the story they've built have made our gifts of words precious beyond all value.

CREATIVE WAYS TO COMMUNICATE "I LOVE YOU"

1. Make your own "mailbox affirmations."
2. Send cards for every occasion.
3. Post something on social media that is a shameless brag about your beloved.
4. Send a ten-second voicemail or audio message in the middle of the day saying something you love about them.
5. Share a prayer journal or letter journal, passing it back and forth.

6. Sneak notes into unexpected places (in suitcases, in coat pockets, with morning coffee, with lunch, under a windshield wiper, etc.). You can even have someone else deliver the note for you, like a coworker or a friend.
7. Look in their eyes and say something simple, like "Hey, I like you."
8. Text them a prayer for their day or call to pray for them over the phone.
9. Ask them when they felt most affirmed by you, and then genuinely repeat that affirmation as if saying, "I still believe that to be true."
10. "Borrow" the words of a song or poem that resonate with how you feel or that represent a memory, and write those out in a note.

Have a good day! I love you.

Get Creative

Texting and social media give you the ability to delete and rewrite your words, but a physical pen on paper really forces you to slow down and connect with your words because there is a permanence to them. We challenge you to think about a truth that would make your person feel appreciated, seen, and loved, and share it with them in this permanent way. Maybe you can place a love sticky note in your significant other's car, mail or hand them a sealed love letter, or try out your own version of "mailbox affirmations." Take the next step to express your love through words.

Chapter 2

SUSPENSE, SPONTANEITY, AND SURPRISE

Take Your Love on an Adventure

The heart of man plans his way, but
the LORD establishes his steps.

PROVERBS 16:9 ESV

Our first date was a blind date, and Jeremy and I both almost bailed at the last minute. We were set up by mutual friends, who arranged for us to hit up the local Macaroni Grill with them before Saturday night church. It wasn't exactly love at first sight, for me at least, but we did have one wide-eyed moment of connection when we discovered that we shared the same favorite movie—*Stand by Me*. If you haven't seen this classic, it's a story about four boys from Oregon who set off on an adventure following the railroad tracks, on the hunt for the body of a missing person who is presumed dead. Their adventure is full of unexpected obstacles and moments of discovery as their bond of friendship strengthens. The movie combines all the good elements of an adventure—suspense, spontaneity, and surprise.

Adventuring with your best friends is important when you're a kid, but it's just as important when you're all grown up. When you adventure with your significant other, character is illuminated as you face challenges; humor is developed as you find yourselves in ridiculous situations; victories are celebrated as you solve problems creatively; wonderment grows as you round the bend and see from new perspectives. What we call "adventures" are simply planned (or sometimes unplanned, more on that soon) activities designed to take us beyond the ordinary of the everyday, which we believe is necessary for a healthy relationship.

Outdoor Education

AUDREY: On our second dating anniversary, Jeremy and I jumped in "OhSo"—his orange 1971 classic BMW that he rebuilt in high school— and he surprised me with a little road trip to Astoria, Oregon. While Portland is the most populous city in Oregon, Astoria is the oldest. Founded in 1811, this little town nestled into where the Columbia River meets the Pacific Ocean was the first American settlement west of the Rocky Mountains. It also happens to be the location where another of my favorite movies was filmed—*The Goonies*. Apparently, I have a thing for childhood adventure stories from the '80s. Any "truffle shuffle" lovers out there? The fact that Jeremy chose this location demonstrated to me that in the midst of all the long-distance letters and conversations, he was paying attention to my life. We quoted lines like, "Hey, you guuuuyyys," "I'm setting booty traps," and "Goonies never say die" while we pointed out where scenes took place. We even have a picture together in front of the house with me in my Goonies T-shirt that says, "Sloth love Chunk." There is some discrepancy in our memories of this day as to whether I just "happened" to be wearing this shirt or if Jer encouraged it. I am so glad we documented that moment, because the driveway has since been closed and you can no longer visit the famed Goonies house.

From there we ventured into town, exploring an antiquated bookstore and a rugged coffee shop brimming with character. Wherever we went, Jeremy spent time talking to the people who worked there, engaging strangers as we learned about the town and their lives. I saw how kind he was to people he didn't know and how genuine he was in making people feel seen and noticed.

We climbed the historic Astoria lighthouse tower for views of the town and ships at sea, and daredevil Jeremy leaned off the edge of the railing as far as possible. We wandered the boardwalk along the beach as we talked and watched the birds soaring and diving. It was one of the last days we had together before Jeremy would return to school and we would begin another stint apart. We savored that day. We talked about the next time we would be together, we vulnerably shared our frustrations with long distance, and we found creative solutions to keep us connected while physically apart, like doing homework together on Skype or listening to the same podcasts.

Going on adventures provides opportunities to learn more about each other outside of your comfort zones, and you see each other's personality and character emerge in the midst of unordinary circumstances. We have learned so much about each other through our adventures and the conversations that followed. Whether it was geocaching, going to drive-in movies, riding bikes, or cruising around in one of Jer's old cars until we got lost, every adventure was an opportunity to discover more about each other. In the thick of it, we were focused on fully enjoying the moment. Afterward, the adrenaline rush fueled honest, refreshing, and meaningful conversations. We found this to be especially valuable in our dating relationship because it helped us uncover each other's true character. I learned that Jeremy was daring but not reckless, confident but not cocky, unconditionally kind to strangers, patient in unpredictable or stressful situations, and always desiring to learn and grow. These traits helped me better understand who Jeremy was and who he was becoming, and they ultimately affirmed my desire to pursue a relationship with him. That's why we believe going on adventures together is one of the best ways to deepen your understanding of each other and either affirm the direction of your relationship or raise a red flag.

> The best adventures don't demand money but effort; the cost of thought and time is rewarded with deepened connection and lifelong memories.

And while this will certainly serve you in the dating season, continuing to initiate adventure will remind you *why* you are pursuing each other in every season! Be students of each other as you grow through the years. We have to break the everyday routine to create new memories and foster appreciation and delight in our relationships.

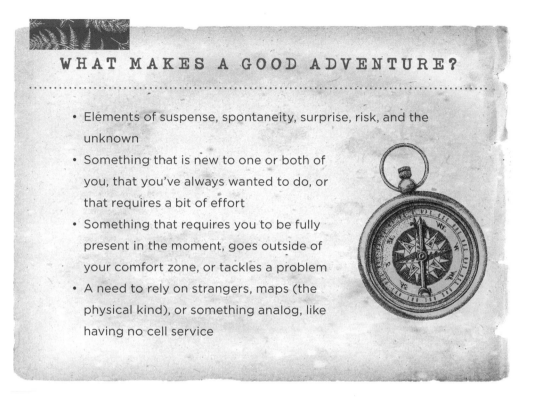

WHAT MAKES A GOOD ADVENTURE?

- Elements of suspense, spontaneity, surprise, risk, and the unknown
- Something that is new to one or both of you, that you've always wanted to do, or that requires a bit of effort
- Something that requires you to be fully present in the moment, goes outside of your comfort zone, or tackles a problem
- A need to rely on strangers, maps (the physical kind), or something analog, like having no cell service

Unexpected Adventures

JEREMY: Adventures can definitely build friendships, but they can also test them. When things go sideways and you can still enjoy each other—that's when you know the relationship is healthy. Like the time our quest for the perfect Christmas tree took an unexpected turn.

In Oregon, some counties allow you to purchase a "tree tag" as permission to cut down your own Christmas tree in a designated forest. We were living in Bend, and it was one of our first Christmases as a married couple, so we decided it would be fun to embark on the adventure.

All bundled up in Rain, our 1976 FJ Land Cruiser, we rolled through the deep, pillowy snow, making fresh tire tracks on the unplowed logging roads. We finally found what we deemed a good enough spot to begin our quest on foot. We hiked deeper and deeper into the forest in search of *the* tree, the one with a beam of light shining down in approval. After a few hours and miles of exploring, we found it! Audrey's toes froze as I worked up a sweat sawing it down. We had forgotten that the distance out meant the same distance back. Shooting each other wry grins at our lack of forethought, I grabbed the tree, Audrey grabbed the saw, and we began our trek back to Rain.

The walk kept us warm, and after I loaded the tree on top of Rain, we watched the snow begin to

pick back up. This was shaping up to be a flawless experience, but the setting sun told us it was time to head for home.

As we were cruising down the highway, I noticed the lights begin to flicker. Within seconds we were completely without power, and the motor shut off. I'm no stranger to breaking down, and at this point in our relationship, neither was Audrey. I told Audrey to stay inside while the transmission tunnel was still warm, and I went to tinker with the motor for a bit. A little while later I jumped back in the truck and noticed the air was much cooler. "Not good," I told Audrey. "It's an electrical issue."

The problem was that even if we could get it started again, we wouldn't have any lights for the drive home—and it was already dusk and getting darker by the minute.

I was starting to envision some nightmare scenarios of my wife freezing in the wilderness. (Maybe it's for the best that neither of us knew she was pregnant at the time!) I'm pretty good at remaining calm in this kind of situation, but I get hyperfocused on fixing the problem and forget to communicate. Communicating with others during moments of crisis is the last thing I want to do. In contrast, Audrey wants to better understand the reality of the situation even if there's nothing she can do to help solve the problem (as in this case). While I desire minimal communication in these kinds of situations, Audrey desires more. Through our many "unexpected adventures," I've learned that sometimes it's helpful if I tell Audrey, "I need five minutes to just think about this," instead of internalizing my thoughts and keeping her distant.

So I told Audrey what I thought was happening with Rain's electrical issue. Instead of freaking out or bickering about the problem, we embraced the adventure. We talked through what to do and decided I would keep tinkering while she'd walk up the road and wave the jumper cables in the air, hoping someone would see her and pull over. Eventually an older couple pulled over to give us a jump. Rain started right up! But then I turned on the lights, and the motor died. We jumped it again and it took, so we thanked the couple and hurried—as much as you can in a vehicle from the 1970s—back home while there was still a glimmer of ambient light. Our lovely, low-key little Christmas tree adventure had turned into a whole different kind of adventure. We had a story to tell because of what went wrong more than because of what went right, and we grew closer because of it.

> When things go wrong or surprises happen, a story is still being written, and how we respond reveals our perspective, for better or worse.

When things go wrong or surprises happen, a story is still being written, and our reaction reveals our perspective, for better or worse. Over time, moments like these have helped us learn to respond to unfavorable circumstances with patience and grace toward each other. The reason I knew I needed to communicate with Audrey on the side of the road was because there had been previous challenges where I had *not* communicated and she had shared her desire for me to verbalize my plans. We've found that if you are willing to keep learning each other's needs and expectations, you'll be even better equipped to face the next unexpected hurdle. Adventures are intended to be fun, spontaneous, or risky, but some happen because something goes awry. In that case you have the choice to panic or embrace the adventure with grace-giving smiles.

Creative Tip: Jer and I learned early in our marriage to expect something to go wrong on every adventure. That way, when the wrong thing happens, we smile and claim it as "the thing," and it keeps us from getting frazzled. This has especially proven helpful when we started traveling with kids. We just expect something to go wrong, so when it does, we say to each other, "Well, this is the thing." And then it prevents "the thing" from turning into conflict.

Adventures with Kids

AUDREY: Jeremy and I knew that we wanted to keep adventuring together once we started having kids. Volume up, parents: having kids doesn't mean your adventures have to stop! They just might look a *little* different.

The summer before Ember's first birthday we took a trip to visit Jeremy's grandparents in Michigan. They live near Mackinac Island, a quaint little island that protects the gorgeous scenery and values a slower pace of life by keeping its roads car-free. That's right—no cars on the whole island! They keep it old school with horses and buggies and bicycles as the only forms of transportation. While we were in Michigan, we knew we wanted to take a day trip to the island. So Jer and I and all his siblings took the ferry over to explore the island on bicycles. We planned to do the eight-mile loop around the island to explore the beauty and history. We rented cruiser bikes, and Jer buckled Ember into a comfy, weatherproof trailer attached to the back of his bike. Apparently she found it soothing, because as soon as the wind was in our faces, she fell fast asleep.

We cruised along looking out over Lake Huron, singing along to our music speaker we brought with us, stopping every now and then at a lookout point, to check out a tourist attraction, or to dip our feet in the lake. A few miles into our ride, the weather took a turn. It started to downpour. I mean, it dumped on us so hard that we could barely see the path in front of us. That's when we discovered the unadvertised side effect of an island full of horses and buggies.

Horse poop. So. Much. Horse poop.

We splattered through huge piles and puddles of it. It flowed through the streets like a river, spraying up over all of us from the wheels of our bikes and covering us from head to toe (eyes and mouths included). We all struggled through for a while until, soaking wet and smelling like a barnyard, the rest of the family decided to turn back except for Jer, Molly (Jer's sister), and me. Jer looked back at Molly and me with hair stuck over his eyeballs and yelled over the rain, "Wanna keep going?"

Having kids doesn't mean your adventures have to stop! They just might look a little different. Bring your kids into the adventure as you write your love story!

With Ember snug as a bug asleep in the trailer, we surrendered to the poop (which pretty much becomes the story of your life as a parent) and pressed on. And was it ever worth it. We loved the ride, and the views were spectacular.

The rain subsided as we got back to the bike rental spot. I'm sure they were happy to see their equipment all covered in manure. When we went to unload Ember from the trailer, we saw that one of the flaps had come loose. The whole way back, Jeremy's back tire had been spraying poop directly into the cabin! Ember had her knees tucked up so her feet wouldn't touch the poo water; she was gripping her stuffed animal and sucking her binky like her life depended on it! We busted up laughing, and so did the employees! We could have been the parents who freaked out and let the situation ruin our adventure, but instead we chose to laugh. We want our family story—our love story—to be filled with laughter and adventure, and that means we might have to deal with some crap, so to speak, along the way.

In adventures like these, we're learning how we can be a better team in uncertain moments. With kids, we're learning what kind of parents we want to be—and we intentionally allow for time and space when we discuss the kind of life we want to build and give our kids. There are little teachable and laughable moments in every adventure story. As mentioned in the "creative tip," this was one of those moments when we didn't let "the thing" that went wrong (whether it be the rain or the poop shower) ruin our adventure.

Let me be really clear—Jeremy and I are not perfect. We fight. We let our emotions get the best of us sometimes. We blame each other instead of the circumstances. We forget that we are on the same team. But when we recognize the thing and call it out, it enables moments bound for conflict to be met with collaboration, patience, and even humor.

NOTHING VENTURED, NOTHING GAINED

Mini adventures: $ minimal cost; minimal travel

1. Have a picnic dinner.
2. Hike to a lookout and hang a hammock.
3. Pack hot chocolate thermoses and watch the sunset.
4. Find a local watering hole or hot springs to play in.
5. Hop local farmers markets.
6. Make your own hot tub: get a kiddie pool and let it sit in the sun.
7. Wake up early and watch the sunrise. (Bonus: bring coffee and homemade granola!)
8. Create a Frisbee golf course.
9. Camp in your yard or your living room.
10. Create an at-home cinema: make popcorn, get your favorite candy, and build "recliner chairs" out of pillows.

Midlevel adventures: $$ some cost, equipment, and creativity required; might involve interactions with others

1. Go for a bike ride or rent a tandem bike (and add a trailer if you have kids).
2. Take a dance or workout class.
3. Go to a U-pick berry or flower farm.
4. Search your city's hashtag on Instagram; find something awesome and go do it, then add your photo to the hashtag.
5. Go to a theme park or fair.
6. Float down a river on an inflatable tube.
7. Go geocaching or letterboxing.
8. Bake something together and deliver it to friends.
9. Take a day trip to a ski lodge (or another public place) just to people watch and eat greasy fries.
10. Take a local tour, go to a museum, or attend an open house.

Big adventures: $$$ requires planning ahead; may be pricey, time consuming, or involve travel

1. Visit the oldest town in your state or country.
2. Go camping, hiking, fishing, or exploring a natural area.
3. Find the closest snow to you.
4. Go on an urban hike. (If you're not familiar with this activity, it's a hike through your city's urban areas, including parks or culturally significant places, or it can be a hike from your city to another city!) Time lapse it with a camera, or strap a GoPro to your head and make a movie of your adventure walking the streets and back roads.
5. Create your own scavenger hunt! Fill it with locations and clues around town based on your own personal love story. (Or check online to see if your city has any organized scavenger hunts.)
6. Rent a canoe or a couple of kayaks and explore a lake or river nearby.

Family Adventures: $-$$$ interactive; offers flexibility; requires more prep and packing

1. Go to a local Christmas tree farm or pumpkin patch.
2. Reach out to a local farmer or dairy to get a tour, see the animals, ride horses, or go for a mule ride.
3. Camp in the backyard and set up a backyard movie theater.
4. Split up and play walkie-talkie tag in your neighborhood. Half the family goes out and hides; the other half tries to find them with three clues via the walkie-talkies.
5. Build a giant slip-n-slide.
6. Play a game of "Bigger and Better." Start with a penny, and offer it to someone in exchange for something better. Then whatever they give you, offer that for something better to the next person. Keep repeating until you end up with something worth keeping.

Get Creative

Share with each other how you would define an adventure. Start by asking these questions:

- ⌐ What makes for a good adventure?
- ⌐ What are some of the best adventures you have been on together already?
- ⌐ What is holding you back from saying yes to an adventure in your relationship?

Then talk through the lists of adventures within this chapter. Choose one you're both interested in, and make a plan to adventure together! How can you invite suspense, spontaneity, and surprise into your relationship?

Chapter 3

STRANDS OF TOGETHERNESS

The Principle of Sharing

Though a man might prevail against one
who is alone, two will withstand him—a
threefold cord is not quickly broken.

ECCLESIASTES 4:12 ESV

Audrey has been trying to get me to take a dance lesson with her for *years*. So far I have successfully evaded this horrible-sounding experience. *No, thank you*. There's a reason our first dance song at our wedding was "I Don't Dance" by Lee Brice. But the more she brings it up, the more I soften to the idea. It's got all the elements of a good adventure: suspense (build up), spontaneity (disrupting our routine), surprise (the unknown), and stakes (some form of risk or challenge—in my case, feeling like an idiot). It's guaranteed to break up the rhythm of our usual outings and give her a good laugh. We'd have to learn something new together and rely on each other through the learning process. This past year for Christmas I gifted her dance classes at a local place in Portland. So maybe by the time you're reading this, I'm a swing-dancing pro.

Maybe.

What really motivated my willingness to take dance lessons with Audrey is a concept that we try to adhere to called the principle of sharing. The concept is this: *if there's something your person loves, there must be something to love in it.* The principle of sharing is one way we build strands of togetherness that are unifying and love strengthening. We talk about the principle of sharing a lot, and we've found it to be a universal concept—people are bound together by the things they share. It doesn't matter what your faith is, what interests you have, or where you are in your love story: building strands of togetherness leads to unity, and neglecting to share life together breaks those very bonds and leads to distance.

The unfortunate reality is, the world we live in makes it extremely easy to live separate lives. You can be "with" your significant other but plugged into entirely different worlds. Maybe you sit side by side on the same couch or across the dinner table but are completely disconnected from each other and immersed in your phones. Perhaps you watch separate shows, do different workouts, eat separate meals, maintain separate friendships, and essentially live separate lives. While this can be expected to some degree in a dating relationship,

> If there's something your person loves, there must be something to love in it.

it can be damaging to a marriage. Pursuing unique interests that reflect our individual identities is important and is the very thing that causes us to be interesting and compelling to others in conversation, yet our modern world has made it far too easy to avoid togetherness. This sense of "my thing is my thing and your thing is your thing" is normalized and celebrated, but we think this attitude is ultimately corrosive to a marriage and hinders it from being all that God designed it to be.

Building Strands of Togetherness

JEREMY: I discovered the principle of sharing in a book I read during college, *A Severe Mercy* by Sheldon Vanauken, which tells a compellingly beautiful story of Sheldon's relationship with his wife, Davy. This book has profoundly influenced me—so much so that I have committed to reading it every year since. I feel a soul connection to the grand love story that Sheldon tells, and I want to build that kind of story with Audrey.

In the first year we were dating, Audrey was able to join my family and me for a trip to Costa Rica—the first trip we ever went on together. If you have followed our story, you know that my family members are the stars on *Little People, Big World*. The show was filming during our vacation, so the film crew was along for the adventure. While at the airport waiting for our flight, we snuck away from the rest of the family and the film crew and began reading *A Severe Mercy* aloud. From the first sentence I read, Audrey's face lit up. I could tell she would feel a soul connection to the story too.

One concept that stuck out to us the most was what Sheldon and Davy called the principle of sharing. Sheldon and Davy asked themselves, "What is it that draws two people into closeness and love?" And their answer: "Of course there's the mystery of physical attraction, but beyond that it's the things they share. . . . Total sharing, we felt, was the ultimate secret of a love that would last for ever."[1] Sheldon and Davy went so far as to read all of the same books in an attempt to know and understand each other completely.

Audrey and I share a love for campfires, books, being outside, making our kids laugh, autumn in Oregon, and farm life. More importantly, we share the same value system, the desire to raise a family, and a commitment to the Word of God. These commonalities between Audrey and me drew us together, but as our relationship progressed, we sought more ways to build strands of togetherness. Adopting the principle of sharing when we were dating has dramatically helped the way we pursue oneness within marriage.

Sheldon and Davy believed that if two people chose to share everything, they would continue to become closer and closer. Hence, the principle of sharing:

If one of us likes *anything*, there must be something to like in it—and the other one must find it. . . . That way we shall create

a thousand strands, great and small, that will link us together. Then we shall be so close that it would be impossible—unthinkable—for either of us to suppose that we could ever recreate such closeness with anyone else. And our trust in each other will not only be based on love and loyalty but on the fact of a thousand sharings—a thousand strands twisted into something unbreakable.[2]

While in Costa Rica reading *A Severe Mercy* together, I committed to take up running because it was something Audrey loved. Since getting married, we've even trained for and competed in a half-marathon together. I can now say that running has become something I have grown to enjoy, and it's a strand of sharing that draws us closer together. It has also taught me a lot about Audrey's perseverance, determination, and commitment as I have chosen to participate in something she loves that has deeply impacted her life.

I also learned to love playing games through the principle of sharing. Audrey and her family and friends love to play games. When we first met, I played games only because Audrey was playing, but now I want to play them because I enjoy them too. I found the thing in them to love—you can be competitive without breaking a sweat, and they are an easy way to invite connection and laughter into your relationship. In fact, we started playing chess together so much that Audrey had a custom chess table made for me as a Christmas gift one year. Now we have

a cabinet full of games, most of which I've bought—something I never thought I'd do! Games have become a go-to date night in for us, especially since having kids. (Sequence and Rummikub have become recent favorites.)

Of course, the principle of sharing will look different for everyone. And we don't literally share absolutely everything. (Yes, we have separate toothbrushes!) But this principle has reminded us to keep pursuing oneness, helped us to understand each other better, and helped us to have mutual empathy. While running and board games may have been easier things to learn to love, there have also been times when we've struggled to adopt each other's interests. (Have I mentioned I don't like to dance?) But when we completely close ourselves off to something our significant other loves, we aren't building those strands of togetherness that strengthen our love—and we inevitably become vulnerable to creeping separateness.

Creeping Separateness

JEREMY: Sheldon and Davy Vanauken had a theory that "the killer of love is creeping separateness."[3]

We live in a world where genuine love—love that lasts—is hard to find. Love can seemingly be alive one moment and gone the next. We see this in the divorce rate, in broken families, in unfaithful spouses—fill in the blank. It seems that love can flee as impulsively as feelings do. Perhaps this is because we are a culture that chases feelings—the fruit of love—while neglecting to water the tree that produces the fruit. If feelings of love endured of their own accord, we would be seeing different results. But we believe that love is sacrificial action for the good of another, and it is apparent that the feelings of love don't last without the actions of love.[4] So we need to water the tree. The principle of sharing is just one of the ways we water ours.

> Sacrificial action for the good of another demonstrates commitment, breeds trust, and produces the feelings of love we all desire.

Continual sharing is a lifelong devotion to ongoing discovery and pursuit of each other. Through continual sharing, Sheldon and Davy built thousands of strands of unity, and in doing so they strengthened the tree of their love into something unbreakable. I don't know about you, but I just love that. What a brilliant picture of two people desiring to get the most out of their love story. Sheldon and Davy's method might not be for you, but there is definitely a beautiful principle to draw on. Sharing will lead you toward closeness; separateness will move you away from it. If you're lobbying for separate lives, you will eventually have them. Where in your life are your actions demonstrating a desire to live apart, despite your heart's desire to remain connected? Allow yourself a moment to ponder this and ask God to show you where strands of togetherness might be built. The challenges of unique roles and responsibilities we carry in varying seasons of life offer incredible opportunities to build strands of togetherness.

During those first few days as new parents, I slept straight through the night while Audrey was up breastfeeding and rocking our daughter. (Yes, I'm a very hard sleeper.) After the first couple of nights of Audrey being awake all night, she started to grow frustrated with my ability to sleep so soundly through all the things. Eventually, she confronted me about how alone she felt in bearing so much of the burdensome newborn phase on her own. Looking back, I realize I could have showed more active empathy toward Audrey during this season. I could have set an alarm or told Audrey to wake me up because I wanted to help.

One night during that first week, Audrey came down with mastitis (sometimes referred to as "the boob flu") and was in pain while also taking care of Ember. As Audrey struggled to latch Ember, through tears she asked if I would just stay up with her. She didn't want to feel alone and was bearing a lot of the responsibility for Ember while also trying to fight the infection and recover from labor and delivery. For the next

> Do nothing out of selfish ambition or vain conceit. Rather, in humility value others above yourselves, not looking to your own interests but each of you to the interests of the others.
>
> Philippians 2:3-4 NIV

couple of weeks, I would wake up at least once during the night with Audrey just to be *with* her. Even if all I could do was fill her water bottle or change a diaper, the fact that we were bearing the burden of sleep deprivation together allowed us to have mutual empathy—something we believe is important for a healthy relationship. I tell this story to illustrate that pursuing the principle of sharing isn't limited to your likes and desires; you can apply it to difficult experiences too. This is just one of many examples in our marriage where we "share each other's burdens" (Galatians 6:2 NLT).

Sacrificing sleep so we could experience the struggle of new parenthood together made it all the more meaningful when we got to share in the joys too, like the first time Ember slept through the night! I'll be honest, I did not wake up every night. But every time I did, I was thankful for it. By spending those middle-of-the-night moments with Audrey, I was watering our tree by fighting against that creeping separateness.

Switching Roles to Gain Perspective

AUDREY: Sometimes the principle of sharing can be as simple as switching roles to gain a better perspective. If you normally don't do the cooking, volunteer to make dinner. If yard work is usually your spouse's job, take the lawnmower for a spin. These tasks might seem like a chore to one of you but a joy for the other. Think of something your significant other does in your relationship because they love it and you don't. For example, Jeremy almost always drives because he actually loves to drive. Conveniently, I don't love to drive. If I offered to drive, I wouldn't be doing Jer any favors; it would simply give me insight into a role that is normally his. It would be less about an act of service and more about growing in understanding. Think of something that your significant other does for the two of you that you could take over to gain a new perspective—even if just for the day.

In our relationship, Jeremy always builds the fires. Whether it's at the campfire pit at the farm or in our fireplace at home, it's never a question of who is going to build the fire—even though Ember loves to help these days. Although Jeremy wouldn't have it any other way—building fires is practically his love language—every now and then I will ask him if I can give it a shot. I want to be able to relate to the joy he experiences through building fires, even if it takes a while for me to find it. Whether building fires or jumping behind the wheel and

WHAT CAN YOU SHARE?

Is there an activity or date idea you've prematurely turned down because it was outside of your comfort zone? Are you missing out on an opportunity to grow in love because you were too stubborn to try something new? Take a risk. We dare you!

Take a Second Look

Which of your significant other's interests do you find it hard to get excited about? Pinpoint one of those subjects and consider doing the following:

- Watch YouTube videos about it.
- Learn the basic rules or guiding principles behind it.
- Read a newbie-friendly book about it.
- Find a person known for that activity and study them (like a musician, player, or famous spokesperson).
- Follow related accounts on social media.

Sit down with your partner and ask them some questions:

- What do you love about this?
- What are your favorite things about it?

- Who are your favorite people involved in it?
- What do you wish I knew about it?
- How has it shaped your life?
- How can we enjoy this together?

Make the Connection

Once you know a little more about the thing your partner loves, start to make connections. Ask yourself these questions:

- How does this interest reveal something that I already love about my person? Does it reveal anything new?
- How could this interest help me grow as an individual and help us grow as a couple?
- On the flip side, how could digging in my heels and holding on to my disinterest hurt or stifle our closeness?

letting Jeremy teach me how to drive a stick shift, these moments have given us more ways to discover something new about each other, and each new attempt to see each other's perspective has tightened our strands of togetherness.

Real life behind the scenes: while these stories demonstrate curiosity and collaboration between Jer and me, there have been other times where I haven't so willingly and eagerly adhered to the principle of sharing. Jeremy likes to watch YouTube videos about theology, politics, "overlanding," and building log cabins. I get frustrated when he wants to watch one of these videos with me because I want to watch something that will be entertaining or intellectually stimulating for both of us. However, when I do agree to watch one of these videos (and surrender my disinterest), I see how excited Jeremy gets as he adds commentary, engages me, and genuinely loves my participation. Although I may not get as excited, I like that I can fuel his energy just by my willingness to come alongside him. I'll admit, every now and then, it initiates some pretty insightful conversations between the two of us. I recognize how rad and capable some of those expedition vehicles are, or I grow a greater appreciation for Jeremy's woodworking skills and his passion for building things from scratch. The principle of sharing helps us grow as individuals as we gain new perspectives and knowledge of different interests, and it helps us grow closer as a couple as our unique interests become opportunities for connection with each other.

Finding new things to love about each other is a gift that keeps on giving. Each shared friendship, activity, role, memory, or way of seeing the world is like another strand that ties us together and ultimately strengthens the cord of our love. The principle of sharing keeps alive the growing excitement of discovery as we not only unearth more to love about each other but fall deeper in love in the process. The more intentional you are about practicing the principle of sharing, the more you will feel connected, understood, and excited about pursing the new version of your beloved year after year.

Get Creative

Of course, in every healthy relationship, people need space to do their own thing. But maybe there's a missed opportunity in something you've put in a box and described as "that's just for them; it's not for me." It might be a sport, TV show, type of workout, or genre of music. Whatever it is, consider planning two date nights based on an individual interest you each want to try sharing. Put a date on the calendar and take it from a "them" thing to a "we" thing.

Chapter 4

LOCK IT IN

Making Memories and Marking Moments

He has made His wonderful works to
be remembered; the LORD is gracious
and full of compassion.

PSALM 111:4 NKJV

JEREMY:

Early in our long-distance relationship, Audrey and I discovered the importance of marking moments and making the most out of the time we had together. One of the longest stretches of time we spent together while we were dating was when Audrey came to Costa Rica with my family for vacation. It will always be a special place to us because we were falling deeper in love and creating memorable moments. We read *A Severe Mercy* together, went for runs on the beach, ziplined through adventure courses, and went swimming under a breathtaking blanket of stars. One night we took cover from a warm tropical rain and watched a storm roll in over the ocean. We hugged as we looked out at the dark, tumbling clouds playing with the sea, and then I looked at Audrey and said, "Lock it in." She smiled, knowing exactly what I meant. This has become the phrase we say to each other whenever we experience moments we want engraved in our memories.

"Lock it in" is what we say before, during, or after some of the most memorable moments of our life together: seconds after being announced husband and wife, while spending the last night in our first apartment together, while holding each

of our babies for the first time, during a peaceful walk on Christmas morning, and after a meaningful conversation on a date night. When we lock eyes and say "lock it in" to each other, it is like capturing a mental photograph that allows us to be fully present in the moment, sealing it in our forever memory, without needing to pull out our phones and snap a picture. In fact, most of our "lock it in" moments don't have photographs to accompany them, but the memories are more in focus than the photos could ever be.

Laced through the wisdom of Scripture is the word *remember*, and the practice of making a memory is deeply sacred. God invites us to create memorials that mark moments when our true identity is revealed. I also love how Corrie ten Boom brilliantly observes, "Memories are the key not to the past, but to the future."[1] We want to encourage you to find your own creative way to "lock it in" during moments of celebration, loss, disappointment, or even just the little daily moments of discovery, connection, or breakthrough. When we mark our love story with a knowing look, a thoughtful letter, a gesture, or a celebration of some sort, we help to create memories that will be recalled over the years as memorial stones in our love stories.

A CONVERSATION PIECE

We have friends who keep a basket of "memorial stones" on the coffee table in the center of their living room. Whenever a significant occasion takes place (a prayer is answered or a dream is realized), they write the date and a few words in chalk markers on a smooth stone and drop it in the basket. In the mix are several blank stones waiting to be written on, and those that have been "marked" tell the most amazing story. It's a beautiful conversation piece, and what began just between a husband and wife has become a story their growing family is participating in.

These memorial stones remind me that our memories matter—not just for ourselves but for our community. What story do your memories tell? What kinds of conversations do they spark?

Memories in the Mundane

AUDREY: In our relationship we think of making memories as making choices, because intentional actions that create an experience worth "locking in" take effort. It sounds like it wouldn't be a tough choice, but sometimes it is. When I worked that first job in Los Angeles after we were married and I had to wake up at 2:30 A.M. to get to my shift, Jer would wake up with me sometimes. While I was getting ready, he would walk to the Starbucks down the street from our apartment and get me a latte. We were making a memory of a morning together, even if it only meant a couple of minutes together and a kiss before he went back to bed! But to make those memories, he had to make a choice. If he had stayed in bed, he would have missed out on the opportunity to create a memory in the mundane. If you want that deeper connection that comes from memories made together, you have to be willing to do things that are often uncomfortable or inconvenient. I love how Annie Dillard puts it: "How we spend our days is, of course, how we spend our lives."[2]

We hope to give you some ideas for how you can intentionally "break the script" and make a memory. For us, it's often simple things like showing up in

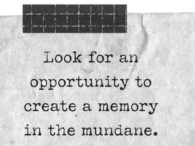

Look for an opportunity to create a memory in the mundane.

each other's worlds, inconveniencing ourselves for the other, or trying something outside the norm together.

- **Show up:** When I was a Barre3 instructor, Jer would surprise me by showing up to some of my classes. When I think back on working out during those first few years of marriage, I will remember Jer unashamedly showing up as the only guy in the class and trying so hard to move to the beat (bless him). Since having kids, we don't get to work out together often, so these memories are sweet. During that same season of life, I would show up in Jer's world by sitting with him in the shop at Roloff Farms (also known as the Men's Crisis Center) late into the night while he worked on his rigs—Fox, Rain, OhSo, or Bertha (which has been recently renamed The Flying Detjen). I'll always remember being bundled up in Jer's Carhartt coat with tea in hand, having a zero-eye-contact conversation while he was sprawled underneath one of his rigs. No matter what the activity is, whenever we show up in each other's worlds, we turn a mundane moment into a cherished memory.

- **Inconvenience yourself:** Some of our sweetest memories have come from times when we inconvenienced ourselves for the other person for the sake of making a memory. Lately, we've been packing up our dinner ingredients and camp cookware and making dinner on the back of the truck out by

the campfire at Roloff Farms. It's especially inconvenient with a newborn and a toddler, but I know these nights will be treasured memories—eating around the campfire while holding Bode, watching Ember play in the dirt, and listening to the frogs and coyotes while the sun sets. The hassle upfront is always worth the resulting joy.

Venture outside the norm: We love our go-to date-night spots, but some of our most memorable dates are when we did something outside the norm. One wintery date night we walked to a local bookstore in Bend (where we were living at the time), got chai lattes, and browsed all the old books, reading sections from ones we found intriguing. Or there was the time when we randomly drove all the way to the beach just for dinner instead of hitting up one of our favorite historic diners. The times when we've ventured outside of the norm and embraced spontaneity and the unknown together end up being the stories we tell!

> Maybe in the end, the memories we love the most are less about something special that was happening and more about how a moment embodied sacrificial love.

Lock In a Good Story

JEREMY: Shared experiences are building blocks for a great love story. The more memories you share, the more opportunities you have for strengthening your love. Memorable moments become a catalyst for future conversations and deeper connection. We love coming back to special memories, like when we brought our babies into this world and the milestones in their lives so far, such as first steps, birthdays, or when our daughter started saying her own prayers before bed. Or to the big wow moments, like when we hit the *New York Times* bestseller list for our first book, *A Love Letter Life*. Or to the memories in the mundane, like sitting by the fire and watching the sunset. As we mentioned before, when we encounter something like this that we want to remember, we usually hug or lock arms and just say "lock it in" out loud. If one of us says it, the other will say it back—kind of like "I love you too."

You can lock in any moment that is special to you, but the following are moments we think are always worth engraving in your memories.

Lock it in when . . .

- A goal is reached
- A big moment worth celebrating is achieved
- You have a first-time experience
- You have made a big decision
- You experience a moment of relief
- You feel a moment of intense gratitude or joy
- Someone has shown you love in a way that's meaningful to you
- An experience far surpasses your expectations
- You make eye contact and are stirred with love

Even if you don't say it out loud like we do, make this process your own. Get creative in finding ways to signal to your partner that this is something you want to hang on to. A few years ago we came up with our own creative cheers that is yet another way to physically represent our toastable "lock it in" moments. Maybe you come up with your own phrase like "lock it in," or maybe you have a special handshake, way of toasting, or some other gesture that says . . .

Let's remember this.

I don't want to forget this.

This is going to be my favorite memory from today.

Recording Memories

AUDREY: Beyond locking in a memory with a word or look, there are, of course, significant memories worth recording. We don't want those moments to get lost, so we make a practice of journaling or taking a snapshot so we can revisit them. There are so many ways to do this. It could be as simple or elaborate as you want it to be. Here are some ideas we love:

- **Involve your senses!** Scent is strongly associated with memories. I bought a special perfume that I wore for the first time on my wedding day, and I

YEAR BOXES

We started making Year Boxes our first year of marriage, but you could make boxes for seasons, school years, or any period of time that speaks to the rhythm of your life as a couple. We literally have boxes that are labeled "Year 1," "Year 2," and so on, filled with mementos from that year. Our first couple of Year Boxes were just cardboard shoe boxes with Sharpie scribbled on top to indicate the year, and we later upgraded to some nicer storage bins with labels that look a lot more organized. These boxes keep our tangible memories organized so we can easily reflect on them while also keeping us intentional about what we put in the box because only so much will fit.

Here are some ideas of what you can include in your own box of memories:

- Concert or conference tickets
- Wedding invites
- Special cards or letters
- Certificates or accolades
- Birthday cards
- Christmas cards you received that year
- Hospital bracelets
- Menus or coasters from special restaurants
- Souvenirs from places you traveled
- Gifts you received but can't use and don't want to throw away
- Polaroid pictures or photos you've printed
- Newspaper clippings
- Special things your children made

wear it on our anniversary and special occasions to take us back to that day through the smell. Music also triggers strong memories. We like to make summer playlists and other mixes for each year full of our most-listened-to songs. Same goes for a special taste, like a favorite dessert shared on a particular holiday. Whenever one of the five senses plays a special role in a moment you want to cherish, consider locking it in and going back to it when the time is right.

- **Take selfie videos** when something exciting happens, when you're somewhere new, or when you make a big decision.

- **Try a film camera.** Sometimes when we go on an adventure or trip, we will bring only our film camera. Then we have a camera to capture a photo of a special moment, but we can't look at the photo until the film gets developed, so it keeps us off our phones and present in the moment.

- **Make a custom photo binder or yearly photo collage.** We compile our most meaningful photos from the year and put them into this big photo collage that we frame and hang on the wall in our home. (Eventually they might start lining our garage or perhaps a barn someday.)

- **Get a copy of** *The Marriage Journal*™ and, once you've finished it, look back through the entries to reflect on the memories you made that year.

- **Make yearly memory boxes.** Fill them with letters, birthday cards, concert tickets, wedding invites, souvenirs from wherever you traveled that year, and other meaningful artifacts you don't want to throw away but don't know where to store.

⌐ **Start an anniversary journal.** More on this coming up!

If you're currently in a dating relationship, making memories that "last a lifetime" might seem a little intimidating or may not apply to you yet. We totally get it. But try doing something as simple as a summer bucket list or creating a holiday to-do list. We did this when we were dating, and of course we kept them. Now they are so much fun to look back on!

Anniversary Journaling

JEREMY: Anniversaries are a significant marker in our love story. We mark out time every year on our anniversary to journal through a list of questions that help us to seal in our memories, growth, and significant moments of that season in our marriage. We have friends who go back every year to the hotel where they got married, then journal through their year and write a word or phrase of intention for the coming year. There are so many great opportunities to use this day to continue creatively building your love story.

We've included some questions we like to ask on our anniversary every year.

You can get your own anniversary journal with these questions and space to record your answers at www.memoriesofus.com. Take turns asking these questions to each other and recording your answers.

This year . . .

1. What goals did we achieve?
2. What has been a high point of our relationship?
3. What has been a low point of our relationship?
4. What new friend did we make that we are most excited about?
5. Where was our favorite place we traveled, or what was our best adventure?
6. What is different about our relationship that you're glad is different?
7. What is the same about our relationship that you're glad is the same?
8. What's the best pearl of wisdom we received?
9. What was the biggest challenge or decision we had to make?
10. What is something we want to do together in the coming year?
11. Is there something that we want to change about our relationship?
12. What's something new that we learned about each other?
13. What did we try for the first time?
14. What is our biggest prayer?
15. Where do we want to be a year from today?

Get Creative

Are you pursuing moments that are memorable? Are you taking the time to commemorate meaningful moments so you can look back on them as precious memories someday? Look for an opportunity to make a memory in the mundane. Collect mental souvenirs by showing up in a new way, inconveniencing yourself, or doing something outside the norm together. Collect physical souvenirs and start your own version of a Year Box. If you're married, get an anniversary journal to help you reflect on the past year, dream about the year ahead, and record your memories. The memories you make now are the stories you will tell over a lifetime.

Chapter 5

POMP AND
CIRCUMSTANCE

Making the Most of Special Occasions

Now this day will be a memorial to
you, and you shall celebrate it as a
feast to the LORD; throughout your
generations you are to celebrate it.

EXODUS 12:14 NASB

Jeremy's thirtieth birthday landed, unfortunately, in the middle of a global pandemic and during the same weekend that this book manuscript was due. In the weeks leading up to his birthday, all restaurants and retail stores closed, social distancing went into full effect, and we were advised to limit social gatherings to no more than ten people. I could tell he was bummed, so I was determined to get creative and find a way to make his thirtieth special. I reached out to all the people he loves and admires and asked if they would send me a video saying something they love or appreciate about Jeremy. I even reached out to some people who inspire him but he has never met! I received eighty videos, ranging from hilarious to tear-jerking, and coming from people who have known Jeremy for different reasons and lengths of time. Then, with the help of my videographer brother, I compiled them into an hour-and-a-half-long birthday movie!

When I asked Jer what he wanted to do for his birthday, he said he wanted to go on a long motorcycle ride, have a campfire, and sleep in a tent. Done! However, I know that under different circumstances he would have wanted to celebrate with his people too. So I took the kids for the day and told Jer to meet me at the farm to

set up our camping gear after his ride. While he was cruising around on backroads, I set up an outdoor movie theater with a giant inflatable screen (twenty-one feet from corner to corner) on the lawn at Roloff Farms. I rented a donuts-and-chai food truck and invited a few of our close friends to come for dessert and a socially distanced campfire.

When he rode out to the campfire pit, everyone yelled, "Surprise!" But that was just an appetizer for the *real* surprise I had in store—the birthday movie! Jer kept asking me, "What's this screen for?" But I just smiled and said, "You'll see!" Once we had our fill of donuts and chai, and most of our friends had gone home, we laid out quilts on the lawn, and I played the birthday movie. Turns out he was able to spend his thirtieth birthday with *all* the people he loves and admires after all. What could have felt like just another day, given the circumstances, ended up becoming one of Jeremy's favorite birthdays ever. I made the most of a special occasion amid unfortunate circumstances.

The timing isn't always convenient for special occasions. Sometimes you're forty weeks pregnant during the holidays, moving during your anniversary, or finishing a book manuscript during a global pandemic on your thirtieth birthday. While a lot of

Find a way to make the most of your special occasions.

special occasions fall on the same day year after year, life happens, and sometimes no matter how far in advance you've planned, your plans have to change. Still, we hope to encourage you to find a way to make the most of your special occasions, no matter what's going on in your life at the time.

Make Your Own Traditions

AUDREY: On the first Christmas we celebrated as a married couple, we were living in Los Angeles, and my job didn't permit time off to fly home for the holidays. Though we were bummed we wouldn't see our families, spending our first Christmas just the two of us ended up being a huge blessing. We've even recommended to our newlywed friends to consider spending their first Christmas alone as a couple. It gives you the opportunity to decide what you want Christmas to look like for your family.

Living in Southern California during the winter had our Pacific Northwest blood desperate for some snow, so we decided to rent an Airbnb on Lake Arrowhead to get out of the city for Christmas Eve and Day. It was a three-hour drive east of our apartment in West Hollywood, so we dug out our winter clothes, loaded up our overpriced three-foot Christmas tree (that we purchased from a tree lot on Santa Monica Boulevard), and headed for the mountains.

I'm a sucker for cozy winter cabins, and this one was perfect for our first Christmas. It had a wood-burning fireplace—Jeremy's main criteria for all our Airbnb bookings—a deck overlooking the snow-frosted forest, and a master bedroom that was like a tree fort inside the house. It provided the perfect escape and ambiance for us to dream together and talk about what we wanted the Christmas season to look like for our family for years to come.

On Christmas Day we started a fire, snuggled up on the couch with a slice of homemade pie and a glass of wine, and spent time talking about what we

wanted Christmas to look like. We talked about the principles we wanted to keep at the forefront of our celebration (like generosity and resisting consumerism). We talked about which traditions each of us loved growing up and whether we wanted to keep them. We also came up with some of our own traditions—some significant and meaningful, some inconsequential and fun. We acknowledge that our traditions may evolve as the years go on, but we cherish all the little ways we've added intention into the holiday season. Christmas doesn't just happen to us; we plan for it, put boundaries around it, and are purposeful about what we say yes and no to. Those conversations early on in our relationship helped set us up for a more peaceful, playful, and purposeful holiday season as our family has continued to grow.

JEREMY: A note to our dating friends: While spending time with Audrey's family during holidays, I got to see how Audrey talked to her parents and interacted with her siblings. I was able to identify if she was selfless or self-absorbed, confrontational or conciliatory, present or absent. I witnessed family dynamics that revealed how Audrey communicates and handles conflict. So much of our marital communication is rooted in our families of origin. When you're dating, you can learn a lot about a person by the way they interact with their family. We understand not everyone may have the ability to "go home" for the holidays. Loss, broken relationships, dysfunction, or distance may be a reason for you to exercise wisdom and boundaries in your family relationships. For those without healthy families, consider praying for a mentor couple or a family you admire that might be able to fold you into their celebration. (We talk more about this in chapter 9.) Regardless of how we previously experienced holidays, as we grew in our relationship and eventually got married, our holidays became shaped by the kind of story we want to tell with our lives and for our family.

It's easy for me to get overly excited about making holidays special. I love how holidays break up the norm and create lasting memories! However, I've had to recognize that too many traditions can end up turning a special day into a stressful day. On our first Christmas, we talked about so many traditions we wanted to hold to, but when our second Christmas came around, we discovered the heavy burden of keeping up with all of them. We still desired to have a low-maintenance, flexible, and relaxing day, and our long list of traditions wasn't leaving much room! We decided to pick a few traditions that are nonnegotiable: making our Polaroid ornaments, writing in our Christmas journal, and reading the Christmas story by the fire. The rest of our traditions are maybes. We'll try to incorporate them but won't be overly disappointed if some of them get missed in the years to come. These traditions include watching *The LEGO Movie*, going for a walk, making my Christmas chocolate beer soup, playing games, seeing friends and family, and (since having kids) baking a cake for baby Jesus. We abide by the "nonnegotiable traditions" framework for our anniversary as well. The two things we don't miss are reading and writing our anniversary letters and watching our wedding video. The rest of our traditions we hold loosely so that we still have time to embrace spontaneity throughout the day and cater to our evolving desires.

What traditions are the most important to you and will make your heart feel full at the end of the day? Make those things known. And then you can let the other things fall in place only if they fit fluidly into the day. If you don't get to them, let them go—you still filled your special day with what matters most.

PLANNING FOR SPECIAL OCCASIONS

Look at your calendar. What special day is coming up? Consider sitting down with your love and making some intentional plans together.

Ask Questions

- What does this holiday represent to you?
- What do you value most about this day?
- What do you love or dislike about this day?
- What's your favorite old tradition involved in this day?
- What two things would make this day the most fun and meaningful for you?

Dream Together

- What new tradition can we start together?
- Choose a "big thing" to do (like going on an adventure, trying something new, or going to an event) and a "small thing" (like enjoying a quiet moment, exchanging letters or cards, or making a special treat).
- What activities reflect or celebrate the values this holiday represents for the two of you?

If you're feeling inspired, consider grabbing a calendar and going through all the holidays together, or find our printable holiday calendar at www.theroloffs.com/pages/creative-love-resources.

Know Your Family Histories

JEREMY: It's important to talk about your experiences with special occasions, like how your family celebrated your birthday growing up, what activities they planned for Thanksgiving and Christmas, and whether they camped for the Fourth of July, threw a house party, or made no effort at all. The point is, you probably celebrated differently in some ways and similarly in others. There may be things about a certain holiday that bring one of you joy but the other pain. Part of being creative with how you celebrate special occasions is knowing your person—studying them so you know what would be most meaningful to them on that day. In light of that, talk about the past—what things your families did to celebrate moments, holidays, and special occasions. Determine which traditions you like and want to continue and which you don't. It might even be worthwhile to share what holidays are really difficult for you and why. The more you communicate about these things before the special day arrives, the better prepared you can be to love your person well on that day.

What kind of story do you want to tell?

Our Favorite Traditions

AUDREY: How will you celebrate this year? Here are some of our favorite ways to make a holiday special. We hope they'll inspire you to make the most out of your special days!

- **New Year's Day:** We list our goals and dreams and write down big things we anticipate in the coming year—travel, work milestones, new family members, and so on.
- **Valentine's Day:** We take turns planning Valentine's Day and our anniversary because we like to surprise each other. One year Jeremy will plan our anniversary and I will plan our Valentine's date, and the next year we switch. This has also helped us with expectation management.
- **Easter:** We usually celebrate Easter with a big meal with one or both of our families. (Unlike Christmas! We tried to do four Christmases with a four-month-old. Never again.) In recent years we've become more intentional about celebrating Holy Week. Here are a few ideas: pray over your home on Passover, take Communion together, make a feast, wash each other's feet on Maundy Thursday, open "resurrection eggs" with your kids, and be silent from 12:00–3:00 P.M. on Good Friday.
- **Independence Day:** We *love* the Fourth of July! Since becoming parents,

we've started some new traditions with our friends who have kids. We watch the local parade in the morning, barbecue with a bunch of friends during the day, and then set off fireworks by the campfire pit at night. Those who want to camp out with us are welcome, but rain or shine, we always sleep in our tent by the fire.

Pumpkin season: We don't really celebrate Halloween, but Jeremy's family runs the largest pumpkin patch in Oregon. Thousands of people come to visit from all over the world every weekend in October. We help out with the festivities and like to wander around the pumpkin patch in costumes on the last weekend of October.

Thanksgiving: We like to go on a run or walk in the morning, watch the Macy's parade, and then cook and eat. We usually end the day playing games around the fire with my family. We did this even when we were dating; Jer would come to my family's house in the evening for dessert and games.

Christmas: We keep a Christmas journal, recording what we did each year, who we spent time with, and gifts we gave and received. Then we paste in our Christmas card from that year. It's fun to read the old entries and reminisce on past Christmases. We also take a Polaroid selfie every year, write the date and location on it, poke a hole in the top, and hang it on the tree. These are our favorite

Christmas tree ornaments, and we are so excited to have a whole tree full of them one day!

- **Anniversaries:** For us, we try to reserve our anniversary as a special day to celebrate our love story—just the two of us. We take turns planning every other year. One of us usually surprises the other, and we watch our wedding video, read our anniversary letters, write letters to be read on our next anniversary, and exchange gifts.

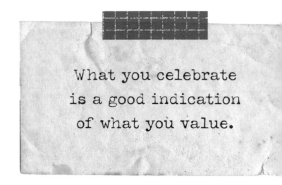

What you celebrate is a good indication of what you value.

How will you make your calendar more creative this year?

Protect Your Special Occasions

JEREMY: When we were kids, holidays were exciting and carefree. But as adults, they can sometimes become more stressful than special. It's easy to get lost in responsibilities and expectations, and sometimes the stress and pressure surrounding these days can cause conflict.

Here are a few things you can do to protect your relationship in the heat of the holidays:

- **Practice expectation management.** We've learned (the hard way) that we need to be careful not to place unrealistic expectations on each other so that we don't put unnecessary pressure on days that are supposed to be fun and life-giving. (More on this in the next chapter!) This is *especially* important on significant occasions and during the holidays when situations tend to be pressurized. For us, we have a simple routine to hedge against conflict, especially when we are going to be celebrating with family and friends. Like most communication, it takes effort and honesty, but it's not rocket science. Before your special occasion, ask each other what your expectations are. If you know what the other person's desires are, you're more likely to be able to meet their expectations, and vice versa.

- **Communicate with family.** You may need to draw lines between the time you spend with each other's family and the time you spend as your own family. Holidays can easily become a time of pleasing and feeling guilty or obligated. You might feel like you need to keep up with old family traditions and events instead of practicing your own. Don't feel bad if you want to do things differently than how you grew up or if you want to carve out time for just your family. This will take courage, and may bring temporary discomfort or misunderstanding, but remember, if you're married, you're your own family now. Creating boundaries around your family while honoring those you love is challenging but rewarding.

— **Talk about what subjects you want to avoid.** Identify topics you just do not want to go into. Politics? Religion? Money? Your jobs? Your diet? Parenting? When you're having your next baby? Some current drama that you know will cause controversy? You both should know what sets each other off or is a hot topic for you or a family member. Talk about it ahead of time. For example, I am passionate about discussing the current political landscape, but sometimes I get riled up on this topic. Depending on the crowd we are hanging with, Auj will sometimes advise me against getting into it with certain people or on certain occasions. It has also been helpful for us to establish what topics we *do* want to bring up in conversation during these special occasions.

— **Don't let social media rob you.** This one is getting more vital by the day. So many of us are missing the moments we're actually in because our brains are occupied elsewhere. Consider turning your phone off or keeping it on a mode that allows you to capture your own moments without getting

caught up consuming someone else's. Auj and I like to take photos on special occasions, but we try to avoid posting to social media until the next day so that we don't get distracted by our phones and notifications.

- **Say thank you.** If it's an especially active or stressful day, show gratitude for the act of service you see your person doing. Big occasions often take a lot of work and planning, especially if you're hosting. Both of you are working hard and probably feel undervalued. Your words of encouragement will alleviate stress, make you more thankful throughout the day, and make your partner feel noticed and appreciated.

Get Creative

Make a binder with all the holidays or special occasions *you* want to celebrate as a family. Print off the holiday calendar from www.theroloffs.com/pages/creative-love-resources. (Tip: print off an extra to tuck in the back for when traditions shift or change.) Write down the traditions you want to stick to for each of those special days to help you remember each one. Keep this somewhere in your home where you can pull it out on these special days and add to it. Think of it as a recipe book for special occasions. You could even add in pages for photos to commemorate each year's occasion. This is where we store the birthday letters we write to our kids every year or any special occasion cards we've received.

Chapter 6

TWO TO TANGO

How to Creatively Navigate Conflict

My dear brothers and sisters, take note of
this: Everyone should be quick to listen,
slow to speak and slow to become angry,
because human anger does not produce
the righteousness that God desires.

JAMES 1:19–20 NIV

JEREMY:

We had just purchased our first home, a fixer-upper, and Audrey was six months pregnant with our first baby. We had planned to finish a mini remodel well before the baby's arrival, but, of course, it went much slower than expected. One month before Audrey's due date, we were still living in suitcases at her parents' house. All summer I had assured Auj that we would be in the house in time for her to settle in and set up for our daughter's big debut, but the slow progress indicated otherwise. After pressuring some of our contractors with "my wife is *nine months* pregnant," we finally moved into our house just weeks before having our daughter, Ember!

Those first few sleep-deprived weeks passed by before I noticed some slight discoloring in the kitchen floorboards. At first I thought it was just the wood settling in, subconsciously ignoring what I knew deep down it actually was. A few more days passed, and it was spreading into our living room. I started searching for a leak, and sure enough, *drip, drip, drip.* When the counters were installed, the workers had wiggled loose the hardline to the dishwasher. The damage was so severe that we had to tear out the entire kitchen that we had *just* finished and redo everything. We moved back in to Audrey's parents' house—now with a newborn who was struggling to breastfeed and a wife who was recovering from childbirth and a fractured tailbone and still battling mastitis. The stress of our circumstances trumped the strength of our character and composure, and we both fell into our own ways of dealing with stress. Audrey searched for solutions and answers by asking questions and processing vocally, while I became reclusive and got quiet as I tried to process the situation. Snippy remarks, frustration, and exhaustion led to a fight about how we take on way too much and never should have done this. For several days we blamed each other instead of our circumstances as we searched for order in the chaos. I felt exhausted and mad at Auj for blaming me when I felt like I had perfectly reasonable excuses. I blamed her for rushing me through the remodel and being overly critical, and she blamed me for not paying closer attention and calling our insurance sooner.

Looking back on this, I have to chuckle—because we still make the same mistakes now. We still try to take on way too much, we overestimate our capacity, and we let our stress get the best of us when things go wrong. Getting ourselves into these situations has provided lots of opportunity for conflict to sift us, teach us, and refine us. I love Charles Spurgeon's perspective on conflict: "Conflicts bring experience, and experience brings that growth in grace which is not to be attained by any other means!"[1]

As we continue to learn through conflict, we become more aware of the importance of communicating our expectations, having check-ins, and establishing our own code of conduct for fighting fair. As we grow in grace, the following things have been helpful resolutions for preventing conflict and handling it in healthy ways when it does arise.

Check In

AUDREY: I've learned that if I'm not willing to communicate my expectations, I'm not giving Jeremy a chance to meet them. So, as silly as it sometimes feels, we have a quick check-in while we're in the car on the way to an event or while lying in bed the night before a big day. We ask, "What are your expectations for this party (gathering, event, day, vacation, date, etc.)?" Yes, it really is this simple. This question reveals each other's wants, hopes, and needs, and it allows us to get on the same page. It helps facilitate unity, connection, satisfaction, and win-win scenarios. It helps us avoid potential conflicts because we know ahead of time that one of us wants to leave early or spend time with his or her parents or maybe do different things afterward.

We've found this to be so helpful in our relationship. Even so, we're far from having perfected the art of expectation management. We still sometimes fail to communicate our expectations well, and we still find ourselves reacting poorly when one of us disappoints the other. But we desire to continue learning how to love each other well, which makes every conflict an opportunity to learn how to prevent conflict in the future.

A journey of self-discovery is necessary for conveying your desires and expectations. While a check-in is a simple practice, the hard work of uncovering what is life-giving to you, how you like to be communicated with, and what you want in particular situations

Communicating expectations helps facilitate unity, connection, satisfaction, and win-win scenarios.

is a necessary prerequisite! Tools like the Enneagram (read *The Road Back to You*, *The Path Between Us*, or *Self to Lose, Self to Find*) and the Five Love Languages (read *The Five Love Languages* or check out www. 5lovelanguages.com) are useful resources. Here are a few questions you can begin with:

- How does your loved one best receive love? (If you don't know, take the Five Love Languages test. The categories are words of affirmation, quality time, receiving gifts, acts of service, and physical touch.)
- How does your loved one most naturally show love?
- Is there an event coming up for which you can practice doing a

check-in? Ask, "What are your expectations?" Then listen intently, consider each other's perspectives, and come to a compromise.

The Marriage Journal

AUDREY: Having regular check-ins becomes even more important when you're married. In fact, the number one piece of marriage advice we got during our wedding season was "communicate, communicate, communicate!" Some couples are naturally gifted at this—bless them! For the rest of us, communication comes with a learning curve and requires practice, but the healthier your communication is, the healthier your conflict will be. If we had to pick one practice for preventing, navigating, and resolving conflict, it would be the weekly check-in we do using our *Marriage Journal*.

I realize you may be reading this and not be married, but we would be remiss not to talk about the impact it has had on our marriage. Inspired by our premarital counselors, after we got married, we started asking each other six important questions every week and recording our answers in a journal. We were amazed at how beneficial these questions proved to be for our marriage, and we often found ourselves encouraging our married friends to try it! A couple of years into our marriage, we decided to turn the journal into a resource that other couples could

benefit from as well! We created *The Marriage Journal*—a fifty-two-week journal to help couples connect, communicate, and grow in love. Each week starts with an encouraging devotion and a calendar to help you and your spouse get on the same page (plan a date night, prevent overcommitting, or talk through everything coming up that week), and then it walks you through six important questions and provides space for you to write down your answers. The journal is designed to be filled out together, so you need only one. Jeremy and I still do our marriage journal every week, and it continues to promote unity, empathy, and understanding.

We often refer to our journal time as our "good time to talk about it." It gives us a space to discuss things that come up during the week that we don't have time to fully address at the time or would be better discussed outside an emotionally charged moment. It helps prevent misunderstandings and mismanaged expectations while promoting honesty and vulnerability in conversation. One of the six questions asks, "Is there any unconfessed sin, conflict, or hurt that we need to resolve and seek forgiveness for?" This question gives us an opportunity each week to work through conflict without becoming offended or offensive, because we are both inviting the question rather than demanding the conversation or a resolution during the heat of the moment. Someday we hope to have a bookshelf full of these journals that tell our love story. If you're married or engaged and want to try this, you can get your copy at www.themarriagejournal.com.

Code of Conflict

AUDREY: Conflict is inevitable in relationships, but fighting is preventable. So in order to better manage each other's expectations and navigate conflict, we asked each other a few questions that turned into our code of conflict.

Our code of conflict is like our rules of engagement for when conflicts arise. Some of the following principles were inspired by couples who are further along in their marriage journey, and some we developed as a result of our own fights and failures. As you read ours, we hope it gets you thinking about your own creative ways to prevent and handle conflict, promote forgiveness, and seek resolution.

Our Code of Conflict

1. **Don't fight in public.**

   Fighting in public usually escalates a fight. Both people become self-conscious about how the fight looks to family, friends, or strangers, which makes the situation more about the fight and less about resolving the issue. For us, fighting in public just causes us to fight even more in private. When we are alone, we can be honest, vulnerable, detailed, and specific. (This rule was inspired by Matthew 18:15.) Not to mention, waiting to discuss issues and frustrations in private has prevented us from countless "night ruined" experiences—not only for us but also for the people we are with.

2. **Have cooling-off periods.**

Don't underestimate the power of cooling off! When we get overheated, we often overreact, and it's much harder to have a productive conversation. Yelling, interrupting, and retaliation are usually forms of overreacting. Typically, the person you are lashing out at just shuts down. Remember: the volume of your voice does not increase the validity of your argument.

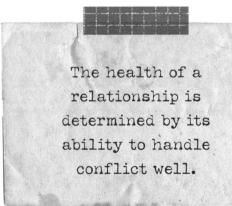

The health of a relationship is determined by its ability to handle conflict well.

Your beloved is more likely to see your viewpoint if it is a response to a frustrating or hurtful situation rather than an overreaction filled with half-truths and anger. Allowing for cooling-off periods offers each person some time to organize their thoughts and articulate clearly while staying calm and focusing more on resolving an issue than being right.

3. **Pursue a resolution** *together.*

Compromise can become a slippery slope if one person is always compromising for the other. Pursuing a resolution requires both of you to hear each other out and collaborate to find a mutually agreed-on solution—which usually means compromise from both sides. Finding a resolution requires more effort and time, but it's worth "fighting" for. If only one person is doing the apologizing, there may be an imbalance in the relationship.

Be clear, honest, and specific about the root of the issue. Avoid using absolute words to make statements like "You're always so disrespectful" or "You never listen." These "never/always" statements create drama and prevent resolution because they are never *always* true (pun intended). It's better to explain why *you* feel disrespected or why *you* feel like they aren't listening. Don't get hung up on "the thing" that caused the dispute in the first place. Try working backward to determine who felt unloved or disrespected so that you can figure out the root of the issue. This is where you will discover long-term resolutions to prevent future conflicts.

4. **Remind each other you are on the same team.**

Our mentors encouraged us to try holding hands and reminding each other we are on the same team whenever we are in an argument. You know that point in the fight where it is about to get bad? Instead of letting it escalate, try reaching over and grabbing your person's hand

and saying these six words: "We are on the same team." This has been one of the most effective bomb defusers in our relationship. It sounds so simple, and it is, but it's not easy. It requires humility, but you might realize it's really hard to be mad at each other when you are holding hands. And when you realize you're on the same team, you can pinpoint what the opponent actually is and then fight against it. Find out *what* the problem is, not *who*, then beat the "other team" together.

> Be the one willing to act in humility and, whether it is with a touch or with a word, remind your beloved that you are on the same team.

5. **Don't gossip but do seek trusted counsel.**

It's one thing to have an honest and vulnerable conversation with a mentor or trusted friend about a struggle in your relationship, but it's another thing to gossip or vent negatively about each other. Gossiping or venting about your spouse is usually an attempt at justifying blame in your relationship. Seeking counsel from friends and mentors comes from a place of humility that invites the question, "What might I be doing wrong that is causing this issue?" Social media and social gatherings are also not appropriate spaces to vent or discuss relationship problems. Your relationship should be treated with respect and confidentiality so your partner can feel secure.

This is not to say that you shouldn't talk about your conflicts with people you trust, especially if you're still dating. Trusted friends and mentors can help you identify whether a character trait is an area for growth or a serious red flag. And in marriage, processing with mentors or empathetic and wise friends offers us new perspective, different tools, or opportunities for us to grow.

A note on forgiveness: Asking for and offering forgiveness requires humility. Saying "I forgive you" is significant. Forgiveness shouldn't be assumed; it's a choice to let go of the hurt and anger and give it to God. Forgiveness is not merely saying, "It's okay" but is an acknowledgment that an injustice was done and that you are choosing to no longer carry the offense. When you forgive an offense, it allows you to walk free of bitterness and resentment. Forgiveness doesn't change the past; it changes how you move forward. A sign of maturing love is that we would take less offense, be more resilient, address wrongdoing with kindness, and be quick to forgive.

Creating Your Code of Conflict

Wherever you are in your relationship, decide what your code of conflict will be.

Take a moment to pray and ask God for patience, grace, and perspective. Then, *without judgment*, evaluate how you handle conflict. What do you do well? What do you not do well? Use words like *we* and *I* to avoid accusation. Remember, you are on the same team! If you can identify what is unhealthy, then you can paint a picture of what health might look like.

*Evaluation: This exercise describes the current
state of conflict in your relationship.*

- What scenarios tend to spark conflict in our relationship?
- What tendencies do we have that elevate tension to turmoil? Do we resist taking time to cool off? Do we resort to blaming, criticizing, or raising our voices?
- When we fight, do we fight fair? When does it become unfair?
- What coping mechanisms do we use when we are overwhelmed? Do we stonewall and shut down? Leave the room? Threaten or attack?
- What do we do well when we are in conflict? Can you remember a time when your partner did something to defuse a situation that you appreciated or that you saw was a wise way to handle a conflict?

*Creation: This exercise helps you determine "rules"
to create an ideal state for handling conflict.*

- What parameters or boundaries can we set so our fighting is healthy and productive rather than harmful and destructive?
- In light of the coping mechanisms above, can you "decode" for your partner what you need in that moment? For example, if

you leave the room, does that mean you really need space to process or that you want your partner to pursue you? How can you be clear in the moment about what you need?

- What can we do to speed the process of repentance, forgiveness, and reconciliation so we don't linger in hurt and dysfunction?
- Describe a healthy way you would like conflict to be worked out.

It may go without saying, but we want to at least mention it: no form of physical or verbal abuse is ever justified in a relationship. If you feel physically or emotionally in danger, please reach out for help. Go to your local church or call a domestic abuse hotline.

There is nothing like working through a conflict and, on the other side of reconciliation, having heightened intimacy and connection. We have friends who are decades into marriage who have said, "There is nothing like knowing that the one you love has seen the very worst of you and still chooses you." Our conflicts have been springboards to deeper intimacy and trust.

Get Creative

Take an hour, sit down with some snacks and drinks (because that always makes hard things more fun) and a notebook, and create your own code of conflict. Use the list of questions on pages 116–117 to guide you. When you're determined to have a sense of humor and humility about your blind spots, you won't get offended. Resolve to talk *about* conflict, and not to get into one over this! Write down a few principles you want to keep, and put this list in a place where you can easily refer back to it.

Chapter 7

THE JOY OF GENEROSITY

Giving Creative Gifts

A generous person will prosper; whoever refreshes others will be refreshed.

PROVERBS 11:25 NIV

JEREMY:

I'll always remember when I really messed up on Audrey's twenty-fourth birthday gift. The gift itself wasn't bad—in fact, we still use it today—but it was the lack of preparation, effort, and delivery that made Audrey feel like an afterthought.

The day after Audrey's birthday was our move-out date for our apartment in Los Angeles, so things were busy. On the morning of her birthday, I still hadn't gotten her a gift. We went out for coffee, and on our way home I pulled into an underground parking lot for a shopping mall in West Hollywood, and I told Audrey to wait by the motorcycle for a few minutes while I ran inside. I returned with a plastic bag tucked under my arm, hoping Audrey wouldn't be suspicious. At the end of the day, I handed my gift to Audrey in the same plastic bag I purchased it in. As she took the gift out of the bag, I could see her trying to decide if she should mask her disappointment and thank me or burst into tears.

It was a pair of baseball mitts. We had been talking about wanting to play catch for months, and the gift was meant to foster future enjoyable moments. But we were on completely different pages. Audrey was frustrated that I made her go with me to get her own gift. She was disheartened that I didn't think to wrap it or include a card. I didn't plan a birthday dinner or anything special to celebrate her. She was disappointed and hurt, especially because her love language is gifts— meaning that one of the biggest ways she receives love is through thoughtful gifts that take time and effort.

The Five Love Languages by Gary Chapman reveals how people like to give and receive love. This is what the Five Love Languages test says about people whose primary love language is gifts: "A missed birthday, anniversary, or a hasty, thoughtless gift would be disastrous—so would the absence of everyday gestures. Gifts are visual representations of love and are treasured greatly."[1]

I don't know about you, but sometimes when I think about doing something special for Audrey, I get crippled by opportunity paralysis and end up doing nothing or waiting until the last minute, like with the baseball mitts. In an effort to prevent that overwhelming feeling, I started asking myself, *What is a gift that would say, "I prioritize you, I've been listening, I'm paying attention, and you are worth it"?* These are the phrases I want to convey to

> When you give a gift, choose something that says, "I prioritize you, I've been listening, I'm paying attention, and you are worth it."

Audrey when I give her a gift. It doesn't have to be complicated or expensive—it just needs to be thoughtful.

Even if giving and receiving gifts isn't your primary love language, if you're married, you are going to have a lot of annual gift-giving occasions for the rest of your life. So how do you keep things fresh and special year after year?

Experiential Gifts

AUDREY: We shared in an earlier chapter that Jer's favorite book is *A Severe Mercy* by Sheldon Vanauken. When we read it *together* for the first time, it powerfully inspired the kind of love story we wanted to live. Jer has read his beat-up copy of *A Severe Mercy* every year for the last eight years. For Jeremy's twenty-eighth birthday I went on a hunt for a first-edition copy of the book. I knew it would be a meaningful, rare, and special-to-him gift. But I wanted to go one step further and add an experience that accompanied this physical gift.

If Jeremy could have dinner with anyone in the world, it would probably be Sheldon. But since he passed away in 1996 and had no biological children, anyone who knew him well would be a close second. Through a social media connection, I acquired the contact information for Sheldon's godson, Tracy, who was a professor at the University of Lynchburg. I told him about Jeremy's passion for *A Severe Mercy* and asked if he might be willing to call Jeremy on his birthday. I knew it would be the *perfect* memorable experience to pair with the book.

I've seen Jeremy cry only a handful of times since I've known him, but this was one of those times. Through tears, he told Tracy how much Sheldon's writings had inspired him, our love story, and our own book, *A Love Letter Life* (that we were still writing at the time). Tracy's response was, "Oh, Van would have loved to know that." Then Jeremy told him that our daughter's middle name is Jean after Jean Davis, Sheldon's wife. To which Tracy also responded with, "Van would have loved to know that too." Hearing Tracy say that was so special for Jeremy—cue more tears. Tracy was incredibly generous with his time, and he said to let him know if we ever find ourselves in Lynchburg.

Have you ever tried to give your loved one the experience of a new conversation, connection, or even a new friendship with someone you know they'd love to meet? Experiential gifts can last in your loved one's heart and mind for the rest of their lives.

Think about what your person loves to read and talk about, what their hobbies are, who they would like to know better, and what they'd like to learn more about. These are all great starting points for a meaningful experiential gift idea that will be worth "locking in."

BUDGET-FRIENDLY GIFT IDEAS

- Find a first edition of their favorite book.

- Frame your wedding vows (if you're married) or a special love note or memento.

- Create a family recipe book; reach out to relatives to get special recipes to compile into a book.

- Make a T-shirt quilt with T-shirts from places that are special to them.

- Give them a work apron or cooking apron with a custom embroidery patch (Etsy is great for this).

- Reach out to someone they respect or admire and ask them to write a letter or record a video for them.

- Arrange a meeting with someone they want to spend time with.

- For food and drink lovers, buy their favorite drink with customized labels (also easy to find on Etsy), have their favorite ice cream shipped to them, or get them a subscription box of their favorite consumable.

- Find the coordinates of where you met, got engaged, or got married (or choose another special place), and have them engraved on jewelry or a leather key chain, or get them framed.
- Get simple, quick things you know they'll love: bring home their favorite dessert or get up early to get them their favorite coffee drink or pastry before they start their day.

DIY Gifts

JEREMY: The first gift I ever made Audrey I gave to her at Christmas the year we met. We weren't dating yet, and I hardly knew Audrey, so I didn't know what she might like; instead, I built something I knew *I* would like—a lamp made out of an old kerosene lantern. I'd always wanted one, and Audrey was my motivation to finally tackle the project. I drilled some holes, installed a socket for the lightbulb, and wired in the switch. To my delight, it worked! I thought it was awesome, and I had a hunch she would think so too. On the underside of the base I wrote, "To Audrey from Jeremy. Christmas 2010. Jeremiah 10:23."

As I walked up to Audrey's house, my palms began to sweat, and I suddenly felt like a weirdo. I thought, *This is embarrassing. I'm going to scare her away—and we just became friends! Besides, this lamp is cool. Maybe I should just keep it.* I imagined what her mother might think: *Who is this guy who's giving you extravagant handmade gifts?*

I turned back toward the car to put the gift in the trunk and save myself the humiliation. I had taken only a few steps when I stopped in the street and thought, *What kind of story do I want? Do I want to tell the story of how I cowardly refrained from giving Audrey her first gift or the story of how I heroically overcame doubt and gave Audrey one of her favorite gifts*

> Creative gifts are not random or last minute; they require genuine attentiveness to someone's life.

ever? This inner monologue was all the courage I needed to turn back around, gift in hand, and walk through that big brick archway, jaw clenched and heart racing.

I pressed the doorbell with a sweaty fingertip. Almost immediately, the door opened, and there stood Audrey's dad. I greeted him, walked in a bit awkwardly, holding the lamp behind my back, and headed straight to the kitchen, where I could hear Audrey and her mom talking.

What kind of story do your gifts tell?

I didn't waste a minute. I pulled out the unwrapped treasure from behind my back and said, "I made this for you. Merry Christmas!" Audrey and her mom both looked at it blankly and then looked back at me.

"What do you mean you made it?" her mom said with a puzzled look on her face.

"I mean I made it," I said.

"What's the cord for?" Audrey asked.

"It's a lamp!" I said, laughing. "Let me show you." I plugged it in, and it lit up—and so did their faces. They were surprised—in a good way. Audrey loved it. She said it was the coolest gift anyone had ever given her. She took it back to school with her and set it on the nightstand by her bed. Today it resides on a table in our entryway. I got to keep it after all.

I tell this story to encourage you! Gifts do not need to be expensive or super flashy. But they should be thoughtful and tell a story. Think about a skill you have that might pair perfectly with your beloved's love language. List out a few meaningful gift ideas that come to mind.

DIY GIFT IDEAS

Here are a few DIY gifts we have made for each other over the years to get your creative juices flowing:

- Make a lantern lamp, a wooden bath tray, an essential oils organizer or shelf, or a hanging light-up sign with a mirror and picture.
- Create and organize a scrapbook, memory box, custom photo book (Chatbooks makes this super easy), or framed photo collage of all your photos together from that year.
- Make a giant kiss made out of Rice Krispies Treats.
- Frame your wedding vows, your family mission statement, a favorite quote, or lyrics to a special song.
- Make a movie or compilation of videos you've taken throughout the year (or spanning your whole relationship).

Giant Kiss Rice Krispies Treat

AUDREY: Credit goes to my mom for the delicious Rice Krispies recipe. I just added a creative flair to the presentation.

Ingredients

1 cup sugar

1 cup Karo corn syrup

1 cup creamy peanut butter

6 cups Rice Krispies

3/8 cup semisweet chocolate chips

3/8 cup butterscotch chips

1. Melt together sugar and Karo corn syrup on medium high heat.
2. Add in peanut butter. Stir until blended.
3. Turn off the heat and add in the Rice Krispies.
4. Line a large funnel with nonstick baking spray, then add the Rice Krispie mixture. Set it aside and let it cool.
5. Melt the chocolate chips and butterscotch chips in the same pan you used for the sugar and Karo corn syrup.
6. Once the Rice Krispies base has cooled and hardened, dump it onto a baking sheet or on wax paper and use your hands to shape it to resemble a Hershey's Kiss.
7. Then use a spatula to cover the kiss with the melted chocolate and butterscotch chip mixture. Let it cool.
8. Use a white strip of paper to write a message. Then place the strip of paper vertically against the top of the kiss.
9. Wrap the kiss in aluminum foil so that the paper is revealed through the top of the foil.

Elaborate Gifts

AUDREY: As much as my love language is "receiving gifts," I also love giving gifts. Every now and then when a gift-giving occasion arises, I am tempted to go a little overboard. Like that one time when I surprised Jeremy with a motorcycle. Yes, that happened.

For Jeremy's birthday one year, before we had kids, I wanted to do something extra special for him. I knew Jeremy had been casually browsing Craigslist for a Kawasaki KLR650 ever since we moved back to Oregon. I reached out to two of his buddies who knew about motorcycles, and they helped me find one on Craigslist in excellent condition.

I negotiated with the seller, who agreed to drive it to Roloff Farms (where we would be the weekend before his birthday) and park it in the wedding barn. I decorated the bike with birthday balloons and set up a camera so I could film Jeremy's reaction. Then I called him and told him to come to the wedding barn for a surprise.

He drove his old pickup truck out to the wedding barn, so I could *definitely* hear him coming. My heart was racing, my hands were shaky, and the suspense of the surprise had me brimming with adrenaline. Jeremy parked the truck, walked up to the barn, and swung open the door. Light flooded the barn, and I yelled, "Happy birthday! Surprise!" He was in complete shock. I've never seen him smile so big, and he just kept saying, "Babe! What the heck? Holy smokes!" It was pretty much epic. You can watch the video of his priceless reaction on our YouTube channel: Jeremy and Audrey Roloff.

Elaborate gifts might be monetarily costly, or they might be time-consuming, demanding, and elaborate in scale rather than price. Whether you have a lot or a little to spend, don't let your generosity be restricted by finances. You have so much to give just with your creativity and effort, so don't be scared to do something elaborate!

ELABORATE GIFT IDEAS

- Make a custom cologne/perfume (We love using essential oils).
- Get tickets to Disneyland, a show, or a favorite band's concert, or a flight to a place they've always wanted to go.
- Surprise them with a trip where they don't know the final location (Word of caution: make sure they like surprises, and consider whether they need to prepare beforehand!).

- Buy a month of workout or dance classes, or get a membership to a studio or gym.
- Book a helicopter ride over your city.
- Fly someone in or coordinate for someone they don't see often to come to town.
- Make a boudoir book (for a wedding gift to your new spouse or for married couples).
- Plan a day full of their favorite things from beginning to end— favorite meals, drinks, people, places, hobbies, or activities.
- Reserve good seats at their favorite sporting event.
- Plan a spa day or whatever their version of pampering for a full day would be.

GIFT-GIVING TIPS

JEREMY: Here are a few ways to keep gift-giving creative and meaningful.

1. **Phone List**

   I have found good gifts come from good listening. I have a note in my phone called "gifts for Auj" (but don't tell her that), so whenever I hear something or get an idea, I log it. That way I always have a bank of ideas to pull from when the time calls for it. For me, this has been super helpful when that elusive bolt of inspiration or a specific idea for a gift does not come easily. Try starting an idea bank of your own.

2. **Gift Reminders**

   Use your phone to set alarms or make calendar notifications for when to give gifts. That way, a week or so before birthdays and anniversaries, you'll have a reminder to begin brainstorming and arranging to have a gift ready! No more stressful scrambling at the last minute to come up with a gift.

3. **Check Your Motives**

   Gifts should never be a bribe, nor should they be manipulative in nature. A true gift is determined by selfless motives. If your motive is to get your way or what you want, who was the gift really for? Gifts are acts of love, and love is never selfish. Take a moment to check your motives. If there is any part of you hoping to receive something in return for your efforts rather than entirely bless your beloved, ask the Lord to give you pure motives. The best gifts (for both parties) come from a selfless heart that hopes to delight their special someone.

Gift Survey

JEREMY: Have you ever been nervous to give your person a gift because you think they might be disappointed or think it's a silly gift or not react the way you hope they will? Are you someone who "buys gift insurance"—saying things like "It's okay if you don't like it" before your person opens the gift? If so, we hope the questions below will help make you a more confident gift giver. Ask your love (and yourself) these questions so that you can give more creative, meaningful, life-giving gifts.

Ask each other (and take note!):

- Do you enjoy giving and receiving gifts?
- What is your love language and Enneagram number?
- What is the best gift you've ever received? Why?
- What is the worst gift you've ever received? Why?
- When do you expect or *want* to receive gifts and give gifts? (Birthdays? Anniversaries? Christmas? Valentine's Day? Mother's/Father's Day? At random?)
- What does giving and receiving gifts look like in your family?
- Are you a "card for every occasion" person or a "gifts don't need cards" person?
- How do you feel about surprises?

⟶ Do you like others to be involved in your special day, or do you want to spend the day doing what you want or plan?

Questions to consider when giving a gift to help you affirm it is a good one (not all must apply, but these will help you in your selection):

⟶ Will this gift meet a need or desire of theirs?

⟶ Will they feel seen and known when receiving it?

⟶ Is this something they already have or have something very similar?

⟶ Will this be something they remember, cherish, or want to keep for a long time?

⟶ Is it different from a gift you recently gave them?

⟶ Does the gift align with a dream, desire, or passion they have?

⟶ Does this gift apply to a particular event or thing happening in their life right now?

⟶ How does this gift reflect the story we want to be telling?

⟶ Does this gift reflect our shared goals and values?

⟶ Does this gift reflect the fact that I've "bought in" to this person and all their likes or dislikes?

Get Creative

Discover what your partner's top love languages are, then come up with a short go-to gift list for each one. For quality time, plan a day out together or a retreat; for words of affirmation, you could collect notes or make a list of fifty things their friends and family love most about them (and top the list off with your own); for acts of service, do something for them they wouldn't do for themselves—like taking care of a project around the house or building them something; for physical touch, give them a massage or plan an adventure where you make extra effort to be physically affectionate. Giving creative and thoughtful gifts is a fun and practical way to show your love.

Chapter 8

PLAY DATES AND DATE NIGHTS

Wanna Go Out with Me?

Enjoy life with the woman whom you
love all the days of your fleeting life
which He has given to you under the
sun; for this is your reward in life.

Ecclesiastes 9:9 NASB

JEREMY:

Playing Sequence in our pajamas by the fire, dressing up for progressive dinners, taking an evening float in a canoe on the lake, or enjoying elephant ears and Ferris wheel rides at the county fair. We change up our date-night activities to keep things fresh, but that's not all it takes to create a memorable moment together.

So what makes a good date? And how can we make dating a regular thing? It's tempting to overcomplicate or overromanticize date night, but the key components are to be alone together regularly and to remember that you are friends *and* lovers. Not every date has to be elaborate or elicit a lifelong memory. It's less about what you do and more about who you are with. The regularity of small "love deposits" builds over time to create a collective experience that is binding and valuable.

If you value your relationship and want to continue to grow in love and understanding, then you have to put in the time, and how you spend your time is a good indication of what you value. Dating shouldn't stop when you get married, and it's especially important to keep dating your spouse as your family grows. A consistent date night is one of the greatest assets to your love story. Here are some ideas for how you can keep your date nights creative!

A Good Date

JEREMY: It had been snowing hard on the mountain all week, and the forecast was showing sun on the weekend. We asked Audrey's parents if they would watch our daughter while we stole away for an early morning ski date. They said yes! So we went to bed eager to hit the slopes and have the morning all to ourselves! We stopped at our favorite coffee shop on the drive up to the mountain and sang along to an album we were vibing on at the time. When we arrived at the mountain, it was the perfect bluebird day with lots of opportunities for fresh powder tracks. As we rode up the chairlift, we recapped our previous run and mapped out where we wanted to ski next. I can't remember what else we talked about, but our conversations were fun and playful. What's nice about skiing, or any active sport, is that it requires focus. You can only be doing the thing you are doing, which means no social media scrolling, no texting other people, and minimal distractions.

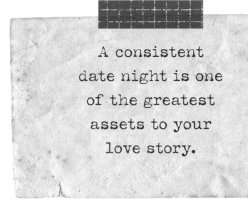

A consistent date night is one of the greatest assets to your love story.

Whenever we are on a physically active date, our conversations revolve around the activity we are doing, which relieves us from the pressures of everyday life. Quality time when we are doing something physical together allows us to come back refreshed and reminded that we are friends, lovers, and comrades—and that we actually *like* hanging out with each other. Our morning ski date wasn't a lavish or spectacular date, but we were fully focused on each other and the activity we were enjoying together.

We've been on hundreds of dates over the last decade, but when it comes to the good ones, we've found that they have a few things in common. So we want to share our "date dos"—things that make for a good date.

Date Dos

- **Put away your phones.** This one is huge! When we go out for dinner or coffee, it's shocking to see how many couples are on their phones, not connecting, not talking, and only looking up to show each other something or take a video. Our phones distract and distance us. On a date night, try to stay off your phone, *especially social media*. Just be with each other. If you do take out your phone, let it be for a quick photo, to use Google maps, or to put on your favorite playlist. Don't let screen time rob you of quality face time.

- **Keep it engaging.** Mix it up, and make sure you have some dates where you aren't sedentary and are actually doing something together. Shared experiences become things you reminisce about on future dates and for years to come.

- **Decide early on if there is something you don't want to talk about.** Sometimes it's nice to have alone time that doesn't revolve around life's responsibilities and challenges. We learned this early in our marriage when we used to think date night was a good time to have hard conversations. After a few date nights gone wrong where one of us left the restaurant angry or in tears, we decided to reserve date night for having fun and enjoying each other. We've found it's better to reserve dates for things that friends and lovers do rather than things coworkers do. Of course, there are times when you need to function as coworkers in your relationship; we would just contend that date nights are not the best time for this. Set a meeting some other time in the week to discuss logistics or have hard conversations.
- **Play!** This might seem to be a no brainer, but we all need to be a little more childlike in our relationships!

A Bad Date

AUDREY: To prevent date nights gone bad, talk ahead of time about what you're in the mood for. We learned this the hard way on a date gone wrong during our engagement season. We shared the following story in our first book, *A Love Letter Life*, and it was one of the stories that people resonated with most on our book tour, so we thought it was worth sharing again here.

Our wedding day was just a couple of months away, and I was so ready to have some alone time with Jeremy for the whole day. Finally, no film crew, no meetings with landlords, no wedding vendors, no premarital counseling, and no bachelor parties or bridal showers!

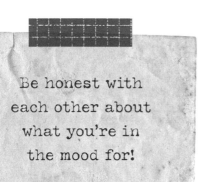

Be honest with each other about what you're in the mood for!

In true Oregonian fashion, we started our day with a drive to brunch at the iconic Camp 18 Restaurant, a Bunyanesque log cabin nestled in the woods at mile marker 18 along the winding coastal highway. They make incredible lumberjack pancakes and colossal cinnamon rolls—our kind of wedding-diet food. While we waited for our meal, I was expecting to have some stimulating conversation about what we had been learning lately, which beaches we would explore after brunch, or what we might do on our honeymoon, but instead I ended up feeling like I was dining alone.

Jer hardly looked at me and wouldn't engage in conversation. He kept looking around the restaurant, and every now and then he'd say things like, "I wonder how they got that beam to run across the whole ceiling like that." I glared back at him.

Are you kidding me? If you had been seated at the table next to us, you might have thought we were on the world's worst first date. I was hurt by his body language and how he was avoiding engaging conversation. In an effort to evoke some kind of an emotional response, I said, "Maybe we should just head back after lunch. I'm tired." But he wasn't fazed.

"Really? Okay, we can do that if you want," he replied stoically.

Where did I go wrong in this conversation? I thought. *Why are we acting like we hate each other?* We ate in silence, and I got up to wait outside while he paid for our meal. Without speaking, we walked back to where we had parked Rain, Jer's 1976 FJ Land Cruiser.

Then he asked, "So, do you still wanna go to the beach, or do you wanna head back?" His question broke me. With blurry eyes I finally looked at him and vented my frustrations. "Can you please help me understand why you're treating me like I don't exist?"

This prompted a long conversation about expectations and communication. We talked in circles about it on and off for the rest of the drive to the coast. One thing became clear: our date had been bombed by poorly communicated expectations.

It turns out, everything I was so eager and excited to talk about felt stressful and heavy to Jeremy. He just needed some time to adjust to being back together before diving into decision-making and deep conversations. I wanted to communicate about everything, whereas Jer wanted to just exist together and simply *be* for a while. We had become so focused on apartment hunting, job searching, wedding planning, and marriage stuff that it had been a long time since we enjoyed doing something together without an agenda. Unknown to me, Jeremy craved that. Unknown to Jeremy, I craved quality communication, not just quality time.

We later talked about a few ways we could prevent the breakfast date debacle from reoccurring: clearly communicate our expectations, be honest about what we are in the mood for, take turns planning, create a date idea list, stay flexible, and make dates a priority.

DATE NIGHT IDEAS

Winter: Heartwarming and Festive

1. Take one of your favorite board games to a cozy café and have a two-person game night.
2. Go to a local Christmas tree farm and pick out the perfect tree to decorate.
3. Go rollerblading (or ice skating) and end up at your favorite ice cream or coffee shop.
4. Progressive dinner: Go to several different restaurants for appetizers and small plates, then end with dessert. You could also coordinate with other couples and go from house to house instead of restaurant to restaurant.
5. Go skiing, sledding, snowboarding, or snowshoeing; stop for a festive hot dinner and drinks on the way back.
6. Get warm by going to a hot springs or indoor heated pool with a hot tub or sauna.
7. Make a Spotify playlist of your favorite songs together and listen to it while you play your favorite board games or complete a puzzle.

Spring: New and Refreshing

1. Go to a local botanical garden or flower farm. You could even plant something together!
2. Sign up for a local 5K race or half marathon.
3. Set up an outdoor movie theater and watch a classic.
4. Turn off your phones for an entire day and road trip to see a new city or town. Rely on other people to find coffee, gas, and get home.
5. Cook a meal together with local spring produce.
6. Rent a canoe or pedal boat and find a river or lake to float in.
7. Go on a nature walk or an urban hike. Take pictures of your journey and frame your favorite one.

Summer: Long, Lazy Days

1. Check out local garage sales, estate sales, or open houses, then go to brunch.
2. Go to a county fair.
3. Find a drive-in movie theater near you.
4. Go for a hike and bring a picnic. Pick up supplies for your picnic from the local farmers market.
5. Rent a tandem bike and ride to a lake or river to go swimming.

6. Make a summer bucket list while enjoying a campfire.
7. Do something neither of you have ever done before—pottery class, axe throwing, batting cages, Top Golf, rock climbing, and so on.

Fall: Crisp and Cozy

1. Explore a pumpkin patch together and carve pumpkins or roast the seeds.
2. Build a campfire! Bring marshmallows, sticks, drinks, and a blanket, and read to each other from your favorite book.
3. Go to a local soccer or football game.
4. Go apple picking and then make an apple pie or homemade apple sauce.
5. Take a workout class together like spin, rowing, dance, or boxing.
6. Make a time capsule together and hide or bury it in a meaningful location.
7. Dress up and create a themed dinner or a "fancy dinner" by candlelight and play music to add to the ambience.

Prevent a Bad Date: Ace the Logistics

- **Take turns.** Alternating who plans dates creates an element of suspense and surprise, and it keeps one person from feeling overpressured and overworked. But make sure you communicate well so you both know who is in charge of planning each time, including planning for childcare if applicable.

- **Collect ideas.** Make a list of ideas on a note in your phone so you don't feel hard-pressed for one when it's time to plan a date night. Changing up the location, atmosphere, consumable, activity, or time of day will prevent you from getting stuck in a rut.

- **Stay flexible.** When we worked in the corporate world, we had weekly date nights on the same night every week because our schedules were consistent. Since the nature of our jobs has changed in the past few years and we've added kids to the mix, the consistency of our date nights has also changed. We had to let go of the expectation of having a date night every week because it just wasn't working for us in this season of life. It was helpful for us to recognize that date night is not as much about frequency as it is about consistency. Maybe for you it's a regular lunch date or a daily walk, or perhaps you swap date night every other week with friends to cut down on babysitting costs.

- **Say no to other things.** Sometimes you have to say no to work, hanging out with friends and family members, girls or guys nights, things that take from your budget, and other priorities in order to make time for your most important relationship.

Let's Talk About Sex, Baby

AUDREY: Yes, we are going there because a good date is a great setup for a good night, if you know what I mean. All you married couples reading this, volume up! Your sex life can be creative too! So let's talk about it. Honestly, we think talking about it is half the battle. Transparency in conversation leads to trust, and trust leads to freedom and enjoyment (a.k.a. more creativity in lovemaking). Developing trust as you discuss your desire for each other is what makes you feel safe and seen, and how you can express your love in ways that honor each other (and arouse all your senses) is an adventure in itself! Making love is not limited to purely a physical act. It involves mind, heart, *and* body. Sex is a gift that God designed to draw us into unity with each other and for us to celebrate and enjoy within the context of marriage.

I've included a few questions to help cultivate closeness as you practice transparency, curiosity, and understanding. To bring greater pleasure to your spouse, you must know them better. As you ask and answer these questions, be open, honest, respectful, and understanding, and keep your sense of humor!

11 Questions to Explore and Enhance Your Sex Life

1. What does sex mean to *you*? What do you think is the purpose of sex?

2. What makes you feel sexy? What makes me sexy to you? (Sexy might be defined as when you feel most comfortable in your own skin—when you love being you and feel desirable as a result.)

3. How is our current sex life?

4. What has been your favorite moment from our sex life?

5. Do you think we have different desires? How do you think we can handle that?

6. What can I do physically to demonstrate my affection and love to you?

7. How can we romance each other during the day in anticipation of making love?

8. How do you like to show me that you are in the mood?

9. What turns you on? How and where do you like to be touched? Is there anything that makes you uncomfortable, or is there a way that you do not like to be touched?

10. Is there something we haven't done that you want to try?

11. Is connecting emotionally before we have sex important to you? If so, how would you like to connect? How would you like to connect after sex?

Have this conversation with an open heart, without judgment, and with a desire to improve!

Creative Tip: Do not have this conversation just before or after you plan to be intimate with your spouse! Pick a random Tuesday when you're alone at lunch, when there is no expectation of sex. Be aware that this can be an emotionally charged topic that can bring out pain and insecurity but can also lead to laughter and a stronger bond!

Get Creative

Look through the Date Night Ideas section of this chapter and pick your favorite ones. Choose which of you will plan the next date and put it on your calendars. Then, while you're on your date, ask each other some of the following questions to help guide you into more meaningful conversations:

1. What's something you've been thinking about a lot lately that you haven't told me?
2. What brought you joy this week, and what is something that was hard this week?

3. Is there something you have dreamed about doing for a long time? What is keeping you from acting on that dream?

4. What do you value most in friendships? What do you value most about our friendship?

5. What is your relationship like with your parents lately?

6. When was the last time you cried? Why?

7. What is something that is giving you a lot of purpose right now?

8. Tell me about the most interesting conversation you had this week.

9. Tell me about a side of you that I haven't experienced yet.

10. What is something that you find most intriguing about me?

Chapter 9

A LIFETIME WARRANTY

Safeguarding Your Love Story

Love must be sincere. Hate what
is evil; cling to what is good. Be
devoted to one another in love. Honor
one another above yourselves.

ROMANS 12:9-10 NIV

H ave you ever bought a warranty for something only to realize that when you needed to utilize that warranty, it had *just* expired? Or perhaps even more frustrating, have you ever needed a medical prescription or procedure only to realize that it's not covered by your insurance? We can't be the only ones who get frustrated by the amount of money we spend on warranties and insurance only to realize that when we actually need to rely on them, they fail us.

When it comes to our relationships, we can't rely on our feelings alone as insurance for safeguarding our love. I know it's not the most romantic thing to say, but feelings come and go, and feelings alone won't get you through the hard seasons, the inevitable conflicts, or the unforeseen circumstances. As we look at the world around us and the relationships that we see failing, so many of them have let their feelings (or lack thereof) break the lifetime warranty and full-coverage insurance they agreed to when they said, "I do." Of course, the hope is that your car won't break down and your relationship won't suffer a crash, but in reality, no one is immune. You need something stronger than feelings to rely on when nothing else is stable.

Falling in love can
seem effortless,
but staying in love
requires effort.

It's the little daily deposits you make that become reliable insurance for a love that lasts. The choices we make day after day secure our love story, and if we don't actively protect it, our love story can suffer an unhappy ending. Falling in love can seem effortless, but *staying* in love requires effort. And there are some protection measures we can take that will guide our daily actions and guard our love story. These safeguards make up our lifetime love warranty.

Safeguarding Your Love with Everyday Practices

AUDREY: Here are a few daily practices to keep your love strong and healthy.

- **Express gratitude.** Basic manners can actually go a long way! Say thank you when your love does something for you, even if it's something you assume or expect them to do. Say please before you make a request rather than make demands. Our creative way of expressing gratitude for each other is with our "mailbox affirmations" that we talked about in chapter 1. Maybe you can try this out or come up with your own creative way to express gratitude.
- **Serve each other.** Even the simplest act of service can set the tone for your love. Offer to do a task they normally do, get them a glass of water, clean a mess, or make a meal. Consider each other's needs above your own.
- **Stay teachable.** Be a student of your person. They won't be the same person year after year. Commit to learning more about them and how you can better love them each year.
- **Show affection.** Maybe you always kiss goodnight or pause for a long hug at the end of the day. Or perhaps you commit to holding hands when you go for walks or give a loving shoulder squeeze or pat on the back that says, "I see you and I love you."

- **Pursue God together.** Talk about your relationship with God together and learn from each other. Listen to a podcast, read a book, or watch a sermon together. Pray *together.*

Safeguarding Your Love with Boundaries

JEREMY: Healthy boundaries within the context of relationships are protective guardrails for love. They keep the bad things out and the good things in. How you set your boundaries will depend on the stage of your relationship. Obviously, the boundaries of a dating relationship when you are just getting to know each other will look different from those of a marriage. You might also have unique-to-you boundaries if you are in a long-distance relationship, if your career requires a lot of travel, or if you have some other special circumstance.

We encourage you to come up with a few boundaries that pertain to the current stage of your relationship. This might mean that you are simply giving voice to a few boundaries that you subconsciously stick to but have never outwardly communicated and agreed on. As you do this, keep in mind that boundaries are born out of humility, not demanded out of fear or distrust. To help get you started, we've included a list of areas that might benefit from boundaries along with some helpful questions to guide your conversation as you come up with your own.

- **Social media and phone use:** Do you keep your phones out of your bed? Do you stay off social media during meals or date night? Are there specific times when you get annoyed or frustrated when your partner is on their phone?
- **Finances:** Do you have separate bank accounts? Do you discuss large purchases before making them? Do you agree on your budget and how you are spending, saving, and giving? Do you agree on your financial goals?
- **Work:** Do you have a good work-life balance? Is there a time when you both stop working to be fully present together? Is travel for your job (or certain aspects of it) putting a strain on your relationship?
- **Family and friendships:** Do you feel like you balance time with both of your families? Do you talk about what relationships might be toxic? Are you mindful of people who could compromise the integrity of your relationship? Do you feel you have ample time alone with your friends and together with your friends? Do you have any friendships that you keep in the dark from each other, and if so, why might that be? Is there a relationship you have that your partner is uncomfortable with?

Pursuing Purity Before and After "I Do"

AUDREY: We recognize that purity is a sensitive conversation, but we don't want to gloss over a conversation that is important to have if you are desiring love that lasts. So let's talk about purity as it pertains to romantic relationships and some practical ways to protect and pursue it.

While we were dating, Jeremy and I won the virginity battle, but we lost the purity battle, so to speak. Sure, we saved the actual act of intercourse for marriage—and we're so thankful we did—but that's not even half the battle. I think Christians especially tend to overvalue virginity and undervalue purity. Purity is less about refraining from one act and more about honoring the other person's mind, heart, and body as you progress toward marriage. It's recognizing that until the day they become your spouse, they do not belong to you, nor you to them. And it's honoring the person who *is* to be their spouse one day (whether or not that might be you!) and not creating confusion or stirring up feelings that will cloud judgment as you discern whether you will be each other's partner for life.

If you're reading this and your sexual past has left you feeling shame, guilt, dirty, or impure, let these words from Mary Pickford sink in: "You may have a fresh start any moment you choose, for this thing that we call 'failure' is not the falling down, but the staying down."[1] When it comes to purity, you can choose a fresh start too. When Jer and I messed up, we didn't give in to the rest of our desires because it was "too late." We started over each day. If you have ever worried it's "too late," hear this: God desires to wash you white as snow (Isaiah 1:18) and to create a new heart and renew a right spirit within you (Psalm 51:10). He delights in making you blameless and pure, without fault or blemish, and free from guilt and shame (Philippians 2:15). God's grace makes the purity battle not about what you did with

your body but about what He did with His. If you repent, forgiveness is yours, purity is yours, wholeness is yours. And in case you're hearing this for the first time, I need to make one thing clear: there is nothing you or I can do to earn this gift of grace. We simply get to receive it and allow it to transform our lives.

As Jer and I learned to make purity the focus in our dating relationship rather than virginity, we came up with some practical boundaries. For example, setting an alarm for when we would say goodbye for the night, finding a friend or mentor who would hold us accountable (and telling them when we would be spending time with each other, particularly at night), not lying down together when watching movies, not watching anything with nudity (together or separately), finding a friend to stay with rather than sleep at each other's houses when visiting long distance, and having accountability partners (not each other) around areas of pornography, screen use, and relationships with friends of the opposite sex with a heart to honor God and each other.

Questions for Safeguarding Sexual Purity

If you're dating someone who isn't honoring and respecting God's design for purity now, what makes you think he or she will honor and respect God's design for purity within marriage? To all of you boyfriends or girlfriends out there, if your dating relationship is headed toward marriage, I encourage you to start asking some of these questions. Ask with curiosity, with compassion, and with an open heart. These are *hard* questions that can be filled with shame or unveil fear, but they're also beautiful opportunities to offer grace, forgiveness, healing, and hope to begin a new chapter of your story.

- What acts of physical intimacy do you want to save for marriage?
- How were you raised to view purity?
- Have you been sexually intimate in a previous relationship? If so, how has that affected you?
- Have you ever looked at pornography or anything that has caused you to lust for another person or reality? If so, when was the last time?
- Do you have people in your life holding you accountable to resist sexual temptation?
- What can I do to help you as we pursue purity and respect in our relationship?
- Does any of this warrant seeing a counselor to guide you on the journey to health?

Wrestling with these kinds of questions will help you establish boundaries so you can win the purity battle before and after you say, "I do."

Maybe you're reading this and have been married for years but never asked your spouse if they struggle with pornography or what accountability and boundaries they have in place to prevent their eyes from wandering. Unfortunately, so many couples never talk about purity struggles within their marriage until someone gets hurt. Modify the list above to springboard a conversation with your spouse. Maybe you need to unfollow some accounts on social media, put away your devices past a certain time of day, limit time with a particular coworker, or stop watching a particular TV show. Sexual intimacy is a gift to be given within the context of marriage, shared between two people for the purpose of unity. We believe it is a gift to be guarded, savored, and celebrated. As the saying goes, you steer where you stare. When you stare at the goodness of God, you won't be satisfied by a counterfeit version of sexual intimacy and love.

Begin the conversation with your person.

If you have stopped pursuing each other in intimate ways because of bitterness or fatigue or just *life*, take some time to address this and ask for forgiveness. Renew your commitment to pursue each other, and if you want some help, seek a counselor. (Counselors can be wonderful resources to move past old wounds and patterns and to write a new script, whether your marriage is in jeopardy or you just need a fresh perspective.) I don't know what you need to more fully pursue purity in your relationship, but I encourage you to begin the conversation with your person.

Safeguarding Your Love in Community

AUDREY: Throughout high school and college I was involved in and deeply impacted by an organization called Young Life, a nondenominational outreach ministry. Young Life values the power of relationships—investing in and building relationships in order to earn the right to be heard. One of Young Life's sayings is that people "don't care how much you know until they know how much you care."[2]

While I was a Young Life leader in college, one of the things our area director always talked about was the importance of pursuing a Paul, a Timothy, and a Barnabas. In the Bible Paul is Timothy's mentor—a father figure of sorts—and Barnabas is Paul's dear friend and peer. My area director was using this example to highlight the importance of pursing relationships with people who are in the same season of life as us (Barnabas), people who are a season ahead (Paul), and people who are a season behind (Timothy). As a Young Life leader in college, I intentionally pursued friendship with high school girls, investing time in getting to know them, learning from them, and sharing the wisdom I'd gained from the years of life they hadn't been through yet. Meanwhile, I had mentors whom I asked hard questions, shared my struggles with, and asked for guidance and prayer. And then I had my roommates who were in the same season of life as me, challenging me, calling me out, and encouraging me on a daily basis. Each of these relationships was edifying in different ways, but all were equally valuable. As it pertains to our marriage, Jeremy and I have couple friends whom we trust that are wiser and more seasoned than we are, friends who are doing life alongside us, and friends we are pouring into.

Do you have someone older and wiser than you who is training you in wisdom? Do you have someone running alongside you who is spurring you on and sharing in the joys and challenges of your season of life? And are you investing in the life

of someone younger than you who is in turn keeping you sharp and infusing you with energy? Having all three will help you grow, strengthen your faith, and gain wisdom in your love story and life.

Seeking Mentors

One of the most common questions we get is how to find a mentor couple. First, to take the pressure off, determine that you are just making some older friends. Simply scan your world—your workplace, church, parents' friends, or friends' parents—and identify a couple that you look up to in some way. Invite them to dinner and ask them about their life. Resist asking to do this monthly or saying something like, "We'd like you to mentor us." This can intimidate people or put undue pressure on a friendship (in the same way telling someone on a first date that you would like to meet with them weekly and that marriage is the goal might stifle growth!). If you have a great time, send them a thank-you note and tell them you would love to do it again!

Questions to Ask Mentors or Couples in a Season Ahead of You:

1. How did you meet and fall in love?
2. What is one thing that intrigued you about your significant other when you first met?
3. What would you tell yourself if you could go back to your wedding day?

4. What have you learned this year about yourself? About your significant other?

5. What bit of wisdom would you offer for a healthy marriage?

6. Could you describe a recent conflict you worked through? What have you learned about conflict resolution in your marriage?

7. What do you love about your marriage?

8. If you could snap your fingers, what is one thing you would change about your marriage?

The same goes for a friendship with a younger couple. We have experienced the great value of mentorship and enjoyed the gift of sharing life—the deep things and the hilarious things—with friends just a season or two behind us in life. No matter how far into marriage you are, no matter how wise you feel, invite a younger couple to dinner or dessert, modify the questions above, and grant the gift of sharing life together!

TIPS FOR LIVING AND LOVING IN COMMUNITY

Be present. Don't skimp on family, roommates (if you are still in the dating phase), coworkers, and friends. Don't be that person who is always on the phone with their significant other while dating, then disappears once they get married. You need community. You need a variety of voices in your life. You need mentors and friends!

Diversify your time. While we believe that your marriage should be the relationship you prioritize over all others, your relationship won't be healthy if you don't have other friendships that are challenging and encouraging you. No one person was meant to be *all* that another human needs. A variety of relationships and experiences enriches your conversation with each other. If you make it a priority to go to the football game, grab drinks with coworkers, or get away for a weekend trip with your friends, you will have more to discuss and share, which can lead to a stronger connection with your person.

Spend time with others with your significant other. When you spend time on a double date or in a group, you see parts of your significant other emerge that you would not evoke by yourself. A particular story or element of humor might erupt in response to someone in the group, and you have the sweet opportunity to witness something new even years into a relationship!

Get Creative

Are you protecting your love? Here is a quick checklist check-in. Mark off each one after you discuss it.

- ❏ What are the helpful boundaries for our relationship?
- ❏ How will we pursue purity in our relationship?
- ❏ What are our consistent rhythms for communication or quality time together?
- ❏ Are we satisfied with our community? Why or why not?
- ❏ Who is an older couple we could invite to spend time with together?

❑ Who is a younger couple we could
   invite to get to know?
❑ When could we set aside time to pray together?
❑ What things on this list could we
   be praying for together?

Chapter 10

DREAMING TOGETHER

Casting Vision, Crafting Your Mission, and Committing to Your Values

Now to him who is able to do immeasurably
more than all we ask or imagine,
according to his power that is at
work within us, to him be glory.

EPHESIANS 3:20-21 NIV

Dreams were one of the first things that Jeremy and I connected on as our friendship began to grow. Over a meal on date night, across a campfire, or on a run, our conversation would always circle back to our dreams—the big, audacious ones, like raising a family on a piece of land we would someday own, and the small, practical ones, like camping in the summertime. As we vocalized our dreams, we realized we were aligned in so many of them—which was exciting and affirming. We both dreamed of traveling for a season—spending most of our days outside and living minimally. We dreamed of starting a ministry of some kind or writing a book that would inspire, encourage, and transform lives. We dreamed of owning a cabin one day, a place where we could embrace the slowed-down life. We dreamed of having a big family and raising our kids on a farm. We dreamed of living life alongside community and our home being an inviting place that ignites meaningful conversation and leaves people feeling refreshed and encouraged. We dreamed of reading lots of books together—over campfires, on road trips, and out loud to our future children.

For Jeremy and me, dreaming together comes naturally, but our process of

mapping the road toward realizing our dreams could be illustrated by the sideways tongue-out emoji face. For many of our friends, it's the other way around. They are strategic and organized with their step-by-step ten-year plans, focusing on safeguarding their goals and mitigating risk. There is no right or wrong here, just different gifts at play in diverse relationships.

In this chapter we hope to offer practical ideas and helpful examples for accomplishing goals that will pertain to the starry-eyed visionaries and the calculated pragmatics. You may want to have a pen and notebook next to you as you read this chapter so you can jot down your own ideas, values, goals, and dreams. We hope that you will be more inspired and equipped to *dream together*.

Sharing Your Dreams

AUDREY: When someone is willing to share their dreams with you, you get a peek into who they are becoming, and that can be a beautiful thing to behold. Jer's and my dream discussions revealed to us a lot about each other and our individual life trajectories. These conversations were affirming and unifying as our relationship progressed toward marriage. I love how John Mark Comer put it in his book *Loveology*:

> Be brave and share your God-size dreams with your love.

Don't get married because you think he or she is "the one." Trust me, they're not. There's no such thing! But do get married when you see who God is making somebody to be, and it lights you up. When you want to be a part of that story of transformation. That journey to the future. When you are well aware it will be a long and bumpy ride, but you don't want to miss one mile. Because you believe in God's calling on them, and you want in.[1]

Be brave and share your God-size dreams with your love. You know, those dreams that you've always secretly hoped for but never had the courage to speak out loud. Acknowledge that dreaming is a God-given gift—an adventure He invites us in to develop trust and joy and connection. Proverbs 16:3 says, "Commit to the LORD whatever you do, and he will establish your plans" (NIV). What a beautiful thing that we can invite our beloved into our divinely inspired dreams!

Strategies for Dreaming Together

AUDREY: While we were living in LA, we began dreaming about quitting our corporate jobs to start working together—it was dreaming on a whole new level. As much as LA was a great adventure, we really missed the Pacific Northwest.

DREAM TOGETHER

- What is our mission?
- Is there something we need to quit or give up?
- How do we plan to make a living?
- What have we always envisioned for our future? What would we be prepared to give up?
- Do we want to travel? If so, when and where?
- How do we plan to spend and save money?
- How can we combine our talents, skills, strength, and creative abilities to be on mission together?
- What kind of transformation do we want to see in our own lives?
- What is God affirming or blessing in your life?
- Who should we seek mentorship and wise counsel from?
- How do our faith and values align with our dreams?
- How can we serve?
- Do we want children? If so, by what means? (Adoption, foster, biological?)
- How do we want to raise our children? And where?
- What do we want our community to look like?
- What are our health and fitness goals?

But Jeremy also had a lot of work opportunities in Santa Barbara (where he went to school), and we loved it there. To determine where we would move our lives was a huge decision that demanded energy and time to process. So we rented a house on Big Bear Lake for a weekend to do our own "silent retreat"; this is where we established some strategies for dreaming together and making decisions that align with our dreams.

- **Go on a silent retreat.** It's impossible to overstate the effect of silence on the heart and mind in this day and age. Taking a weekend or twenty-four-hour silent retreat will give you clarity for dream discerning, goal setting, or making a hard decision. Silence gives you a chance to really think.

- **Use butcher paper lists.** We're big into pro and con lists for decision-making and goal-mapping our dreams. Having this visually represented on wide-format paper helps us compare, whittle down, redirect, and synthesize ideas where we need to—a huge bonus for visual learners like us! If butcher paper isn't your thing, you could do this same practice with a dry-erase board, Google Docs, or a plain old-fashioned notebook.

- **Set deadlines and timelines.** Deciding *when* you are going to make a big decision or achieve a goal gives you an end date, so you don't carry anxiety for an indeterminate time. Are there any big decisions hanging over your head? List them and set some deadlines today. Having an end point is a huge weight off your shoulders.

- **Create a dream journal.** Start a joint journal and write down things you are working toward—big goals, small goals, or decisions you have to make. This can also be a space where you write down what you have accomplished as a couple. Reflect back through the pages to assess how your life is lining up with the pursuit of your dreams.

Marriage Summits

AUDREY: A few years ago some of our mentors, Chris and Jamie Herb, invited us (and a few other couples) into the sacred practice of a marriage summit. We managed to break away for the weekend, and they led us through their annual process of evaluating and setting goals for their marriage that align with their marriage mission and family values. We loved it so much that we have adopted this annual practice, and if you're married, we hope that you will as well.

So what do you do at a marriage summit?

- Assess the present reality of your marriage.
- Discuss the ideal state of your marriage.
- Set goals for the year and check in on long-term goals.
- Reevaluate your marriage mission statement and family values (or create them if you never have).
- Determine steps to make course corrections where they are needed.

On our marriage summits we talk about the greatest challenge we are currently facing as a couple, our major victories from the year, and big things we anticipate in the coming year. We discuss something we want to continue doing and something we want to return to. During our first marriage summit we crafted our own marriage mission statement and established our family values. Each year since then has served as a time to revisit them, making sure we're on the right path and correcting course if needed.

One of the most eye-opening practices we learned on our first marriage summit with the Herbs was writing our "current reality vs. ideal state." Prior to our marriage summit, the Herbs had asked both of us to individually (without discussion) write out our "ideal state" and then write our "reality state" for each of the following aspects of our marriage: communication, finances, spiritual health, and physical intimacy/sex. Then during the retreat we took time as a couple to write our merged vision for the "ideal state" for each category.

Here is the prompt for you that you can adapt for each category:

In a few sentences, write, using the present tense, the "ideal state" of the health of your communication in your marriage. (Be specific about your communication styles and conflict styles.) Then, in as many sentences needed, from your perspective, write out the current reality of the health of your communication in your marriage relationship. Once you've done this separately, read each other your "current realities" and "ideal states." Then use both of your "ideal states" to develop a joint "ideal state."

- **Communication:** evaluate communication styles (verbal and nonverbal), expectations, conflict styles, apologies, and tone of voice.
- **Financial health:** evaluate things like generosity, investments, communication about large and small expenses, and financial goals (e.g., vacations, supporting a cause, paying off debt).
- **Spiritual health:** evaluate things like time with the Lord, prayer, community, wise counsel, and connecting with each other on faith.
- **Physical intimacy:** evaluate things like frequency, initiation, and freedom in communication.

Here is an example from one of our marriage retreats to give you a better idea of what this practice looks like:

Audrey's current reality for communication: "We have a hard time communicating about things that will take a while to talk through because we don't have time to really sit down and work through them. We brush a lot under the rug; we are often snappy with each other, but we are always honest. Our communication styles are different, which can be a huge blessing at times but a challenge at other times. We have skipped weeks of our marriage journal lately and miss out on resolving conversations that we started throughout the week. We do talk with each other all day long though, because we work together, which requires a lot of communication about decisions and scheduling, but sometimes it's hard to get past that and set aside time for the more meaningful conversations."

Jeremy and Audrey's ideal state of communication: "We communicate in an encouraging, patient, and affirming way based on our love languages and what we've learned about each other from the Enneagram. We do our marriage journal every Sunday night, and if we have a scheduling conflict, we do it early Monday morning. We put our phones down and make eye contact during important discussions. We value honesty and confront conflict with compassion while also being sensitive to the timing."

The idea is that you write your current realities separately because they may be different based on each of your perspectives. But then you review them together and write your ideal state (in the present tense to help visualize it as a reality) of what you are agreeing on pursuing together.

Craft a Marriage Mission Statement

JEREMY: Every successful sports team, organization, church, and business has a mission statement, goals, and yearly summits, yet how many of us just leave our marriages up to chance? Why don't we treat our family with the same intentionality? Why don't we plan for success when it comes to our marriage?

Having your own marriage or family mission statement will help clarify your values, purpose, and vision. If you have a copy of *The Marriage Journal*, the opening section has a space for writing your marriage mission statement. This is our marriage mission statement:

> We want our marriage to be a creative representation of the love of Christ that is refreshing, inviting, and igniting. We want to inspire our generation to be more intentional with their work, relationships, and life.

What might your marriage mission statement include? Consider the following questions, then write your statement.

→ What do we want other people to learn from, gain, or see when they look at our marriage?

→ What kind of impact do we want to leave on the world? How do we want to add to the lives of others?

→ What is it about our love in particular that we most want to share with others?

Determining Your Family Values

JEREMY: What do you want your family to ultimately be about? What are the pillars that you want to guide you day to day and that you want to stand for through all the changing seasons of life? These values are the things that hold up your life; they represent your deepest values, as opposed to your desires. A *value* is something that guides you over the long term, while a *desire* may come and go. For example, you may have the *value* that you want to be healthy and eat nutritious whole foods but have the *desire* for a Reese's Blizzard from DQ. In this predicament, having pre-established values or pillars will help to guide your decisions so that your strongest desires in the moment (hello, creamy goodness) won't overcome your deepest desires (long-term health).

We are sharing ours with you as an example in the hope of inspiring you to come up with your own unique-to-you family values:

> Family values will help guide your decisions.

- **Apprenticeship to Jesus:** We want to be with Jesus, be like Jesus, and do what He did. We study His Word and life on our own, together, and in community with others.

- **Family:** We love each other through serving, encouraging, playing, and learning together. We prioritize our relationships with each other and commit to honesty and forgiveness.

- **Adventure:** We choose to embrace the intentional and unintentional adventures that life presents. We are adaptable, willing to try new things, and excited to discover more about each other as we share new experiences together.

- **Community and wise counsel:** We believe in love-drenched accountability through close fellowship with like-minded disciples of Jesus. We have teachable hearts and seek wisdom and insight from those who are older than us and whose lives bear much fruit.

- **Health and wellness:** We are intentional about what we put in and on our bodies, and we are gatekeepers of our home. We aim to live naturally and avoid exposure to toxins by educating ourselves about products, consumables, and medicines. We try to get outside every day, and we care for our bodies by being physically active.

- **The table:** Jesus did some of His most important work around a table, so we commit to having table time and sharing meals with family and community on a regular basis. We practice hospitality within our own family and with anyone who comes into our home.

- **A creative, intentional, faithful marriage:** Our marriage is an example of the creativity, intention, and faithfulness of God. We pursue each other and aim to outdo each other in showing honor. We adhere to the principle of sharing, and we always seek to show more love and respect toward each other in ever-fresh ways.

- **Stewardship and generosity:** We are blessed to be a blessing and recognize that all we have is given to us by God. We wisely steward what we have been given and submit our finances to the Lord. We are quick to give away what we have to meet the needs of others, and we always look for opportunities to be more generous with our resources, time, and finances.

- **Rest and sabbath:** We believe that love, joy, and peace are incompatible with hurry. We were designed to rest, so we practice the sabbath in an effort to align with the heartbeat of God. On the Sabbath, we stop scrolling, spending, and working. We spend time with people we love, do things we enjoy, and worship the living God.

⟶ **Work and creating:** All that we do, say, and represent is with the intent of demonstrating the love of Christ, carrying out the Great Commission, and inspiring and igniting hearts to walk with Jesus. We want to always be creating in some capacity and don't want to be idle unless for a season of rest.

Now talk about the principles, practices, and priorities you want to have as a family, and come up with a sentence or two describing each one. Then write them down and keep them somewhere you can reference easily. It might be helpful to ask questions like these:

⟶ What is most important to us as a family?

⟶ What do we want to be known for? What are our priorities?

⟶ What would we feel constitutes a healthy, balanced life?

⟶ What are our gifts and talents?

⟶ In what areas of our life have we been affirmed?

⟶ What doors has God opened or shut?

Nailing down your family values might seem like a bit of a daunting task, but honestly, one intentional planning session will serve as a beautiful framework for years to come.

Get Creative

Two people pursuing creative love can be a powerful and world-changing force. If you're dating, sit around a campfire or go on a picnic, talk about your dreams, and see if you're headed in the same direction. If you're married, consider planning a summit for the two of you to dedicate time to your dreams and goals. Align your resources, get excited, and make plans. It can be as simple as a day spent at home or a full-on getaway. Determine a date and mark your calendar now! If you have never crafted a marriage mission statement or your family values, do this on your first marriage summit and print them off or turn them into art that you could hang in your home as a beautiful reminder of what you want to be about as a couple and family. Your mission statement and values will help to guide your decisions and goals as you continue to dream together for life!

Notes

Chapter 3: Strands of Togetherness

1. Sheldon Vanauken, *A Severe Mercy* (San Francisco: HarperSanFrancisco, 1987), 35.
2. Vanauken, *Severe Mercy*, 35.
3. Vanauken, *Severe Mercy*, 37.
4. Timothy Keller, *The Meaning of Marriage: Facing the Complexities of Commitment with the Wisdom of God* (New York: Riverhead, 2011), 109.

Chapter 4: Lock It In

1. Corrie ten Boom, *The Hiding Place* (Peabody, MA: Hendrickson, 2009), 17.
2. Annie Dillard, *The Writing Life* (New York: HarperCollins, 1989), 32.

Chapter 6: Two to Tango

1. Charles H. Spurgeon, *The Complete Works of C. H. Spurgeon*, vol. 52, *Sermons 2968–3019* (Harrington, DE: Delmarva Publications, 2013), n.p.

Chapter 7: The Joy of Generosity

1. "Receiving Gifts," *The 5 Love Languages*, accessed May 11, 2020, https://www.5lovelanguages.com/languages/receiving-gifts/.

Chapter 9: A Lifetime Warranty

1. Mary Pickford, *Why Not Try God?* (1934; repr., Culver City, CA: Northern Road, 2013), 26.
2. "Every Story Matters," Young Life, accessed May 15, 2020, https://mthoreb.younglife.org/find-us/.

Chapter 10: Dreaming Together

1. John Mark Comer, *Loveology: God, Love, Marriage, Sex, and the Never-Ending Story of Male and Female* (Grand Rapids: Zondervan, 2013), 72, italics original.

About the Authors

JEREMY AND AUDREY ROLOFF are the founders of Beating50Percent, an online marriage community that provides resources, ignites conversations, and offers encouraging content to inspire and equip marriages. They cohost a top-charting podcast called *Behind the Scenes*, are the *New York Times* bestselling authors of *A Love Letter Life*, are founders of *The Marriage Journal*, and are former costars of the longest-running family reality television show in history, *Little People, Big World*. Jeremy loves old cars and campfires and is always working on a DIY project. Audrey loves running and all things floral and is passionate about natural, healthy living. The Roloffs live in Oregon with their daughter, Ember, and son, Bode. To learn more about Jeremy and Audrey, go to www.theroloffs.com.